Master/slave Mastery
Updated handbook of concepts, approaches and practices

by Robert J. Rubel Ph.D.
and
M. Jen Fairfield

Other Books by Robert J. Rubel (Dr. Bob)

Master/slave Relations: Handbook of Theory and Practice

This book was totally revised and is now available as: Master/slave Mastery: Updated handbook of concepts, approaches, and practices by Robert J. Rubel, Ph.D. and M. Jen Fairfield (2014)

Protocols Handbook for the Leather slave: Theory and Practice

(This is the gender-free version of Protocols: Handbook for the Female slave) More than a book of traditional Leather protocols, this book demonstrates how to use protocols to make your particular relationship magical. This book is intended to suggest protocols that you, yourself, will adapt to your particular structure.

Master/slave Relations: Communications 401–the advanced course

All relationships have communication challenges, and many of these challenges are amplified when living in a structured relationship. This book teases out some of communication glitches that are often hard to identify and modify even in vanilla relationships. This book is written specifically for couples living in a D/s or M/s structure where there are certain constraints when speaking with one another.

Master/slave Relations: Solutions 402–living in harmony

If you're sensing that one of you is growing apart from the other, if you are concerned that one or more of your core values may be different from your partner and you want to work on growing back together, this is your book. It's really a book of things to think/talk about that will strengthen your relationship.

Squirms, Screams, and Squirts: Handbook for going from great sex to extraordinary sex

Most men want to be good lovers. Most men want to please their female partners. Unfortunately, exactly how to please a female lover is a mystery to many men—and good instruction is very difficult to find. In fact, I wrote this book because I was not satisfied with the books that I could find on the subject. Here, in this one volume, is absolutely first-rate information about the who, what, where, when, why, and how of creating an intensely pleasurable sexual experience for a woman.

All published by Nazca Plains, Las Vegas, Nevada. You can purchase these books through Amazon.

Signed copies are available directly from Jen and Dr. Bob through their website, *www.KinkMastery.com*

Dear Readers –

There are two troubling aftereffects that arise when I write a book. Actually, these aftereffects arise when anyone in our BDSM community writes a book.

First, some readers will read only part of the book, focus on points they object to, and then speak widely about how this writer doesn't have a clue about how things are really done rather than read through the material with an eye to adapting concepts and ideas that speak to them.

Second, written words lock an author's thoughts into place in peoples' minds. Authors get associated with certain viewpoints and it can be quite challenging to get previous readers to understand that you, the author, have broadened your understanding of a topic over the span of years.

This second point is important, for reading a book is rather like looking at a snapshot: this is a slice of material representing our viewpoints at this time. The same photographer/writer working with similar material five years into the future will produce a different image or book. That's understandable, as they've learned more over time.

I have learned a great deal about BDSM and Master/slave material since my last books in the 2006-7 period. I hope you enjoy the differences.

– Robert J. (Dr. Bob) Rubel

A servant serves Master's needs or is fired;
A slave serves Master's wants or is released.

However, Master's wants must not trump slave's needs,
Even when playing by RACK standards.

slave is in service to Master;
However, Master is in service to the relationship.

Welcome to the complex and elegant
World of Master/slave relations.

Other Books by Robert J. Rubel and M. Jen Fairfield

*BDSM Mastery—Basics: your guide
to play, parties, and scene protocols*
(Book One in the BDSM Mastery Series)
2014

*BDSM Mastery—Relationships: a guide for creating
mindful relationships for Dominants and submissives*
(Book Two in the BDSM Mastery Series)
2014

*Master/slave Mastery:
Refining the fire—ideas that matter*
(Book Two in the Master/slave Mastery Series)
2015

Books are published by Red Eight Ball Press, Austin, TX and are available through Amazon. Signed copies are available through our website *www.KinkMastery.com*

Master/slave Mastery
Updated handbook of concepts, approaches and practices

by Robert J. Rubel Ph.D.
and
M. Jen Fairfield

Red 8 Ball Press

www.KinkMastery.com

Red Eight Ball Press
P.O. Box 171303
Austin, TX 78717

Master/slave Mastery
Updated handbook of concepts, approaches and practices

© 2014 by Robert J. Rubel and M. Jen Fairfield
ISBN 978-0-9863521-1-9

Cover Design: M. Jen Fairfield and RhodesCreativeStudio

Library of Congress Catalog Number: 2014959366

Published by Red Eight Ball Press
Printed in the United States of America

This book is dedicated to Robert Steele who, just to prove that he could, decided to create me.

This book certainly would not exist without his help and support over the years. He remains one of my closest friends to this day.

Preface

Jen and I have been working on this book and its three associated books for over two years. I'd like to share our point of view with you and explain how these four books tie in with one another.

We consider the body of knowledge needed to understand the worlds of BDSM to be different from the body of knowledge needed to understand the worlds of Masters and slaves. The reason they are so different lies in the distinction commonly made between a submissive and a slave. After countless conversations with Masters, Dom/mes, submissives and slaves, we've come to the conclusion that the role of a submissive is a voluntary position; the submissive generally retains the right to tell their Dom/me "no." On the other hand, a slave is owned property and has surrendered power over itself in exchange for total protection and leadership by his or her Master. Thus, the "rules of engagement" are fundamentally different for couples in a D/s relationship and for couples in an M/s relationship. In an effort to capture those differences, we wrote two books in the BDSM Mastery series and two books in the Master/slave Mastery series.

The first BDSM Mastery book *(BDSM Mastery–Basics: your guide to play, parties, and scene protocols)* covers about everything we could think of except **relationship** topics. We saved all the relationship material for the second book *(BDSM Mastery–Relationships: a guide for creating mindful relationships for Dominants and submissives).*

Similarly, we divided the Master/slave Mastery series into two books. This is the first of the two and it is a rewrite and substantial expansion of my previous book, *Master/slave Relations: Handbook of theory and practice (2006)*. Now: the second book in this current series is quite different from any I have previously written. It's an advanced book for Masters and slaves and covers the difficult topics you run into after living M/s for many years. Also, it includes excerpts, notes, and ideas from the dozens and dozens of M/s-related workshops I've attended since I began going to weekend kink conferences in 2004. As I've been active on the national lecture circuit since 2007, I've had the amazing opportunity to hear most of the senior Masters discuss their take on this topic. As I'm an inveterate note-taker, I've been accumulated a huge amount of material over the years. It is that material, plus my own observations, that has been poured into that second book in the *Master/slave Mastery series*. It is, in fact, a book about *Exploring M/s with intent.*

Both Jen and I hope you enjoy all these books as much as we have enjoyed putting them together.

Robert J. (Dr. Bob) Rubel and M. Jen (Jen) Fairfield

Table of Contents

Table of Contents

Chapter 1
Getting Started

When I first discovered the world of BDSM in 2001—a world filled with new words such as Tops, bottoms, Dominants, submissives, Masters, Owners, slaves, and property—I asked many, many people what these words meant. I was left with the general impression that nobody really had a grip on how these words differed: they were guessing, based primarily on how they, themselves, used the terms and what they had picked up from socializing with others within their (small) BDSM communities who were similarly guessing about what the words meant.

Repeatedly, I was told that Master/slave (M/s) relationships were simply a more extreme version of Dominant/submissive (D/s) relationships. Many people suggested that M/s and D/s were really the same thing and used the words interchangeably. "That's interesting," I thought. "Probably wrong, but interesting." To my mind, calling a table a chair doesn't make it one.

But what did I know? Though I was 56 at the time, I had no prior BDSM experience. But, I'm a word guy as well as an educational sociologist, so I began to wonder whether I could put parameters around these terms, if only to be able to speak clearly to others about the psychological aspect of BDSM. After all, the middle letters of BDSM are DS—Dominance and submission.

So I dug further and discovered that some people are more qualified than others to discuss D/s, M/s, and O/p: I discovered that in the same way that there are weekend BDSM conferences and weekend rope conferences, there are weekend Master/slave conferences. Finally, by about 2003, I found two Leather Masters (Master Steve Sampson and Master Skip Chasey), who at a weekend conference described Top/bottom as being about the *physical body,* D/s as being about the *mental body*, and M/s as being about the *spiritual body*. It took some time before I understood the implications of those distinctions.

As in all technical fields, you have to know a lot before you can understand the advanced material.

That brings us to *this* book.

This book is the first in a series of books devoted to Master/slave mastery. Yes, I've written other books on Master/slave topics, but that was in the 2006-7 period and I've learned so much since then that this series updates and expands those ideas. This is the first book in this new series, and it's designed to give you a thorough understanding not only the intricacies of the Master/slave dynamic, but also how vastly different M/s is from D/s. This series of books are designed both to demystify this topic and to give you the tools and knowledge to explore this small sub-culture that lives within the overall BDSM culture.

So, for the sake of keeping them straight as you read this book, let me start out by drawing a clear distinction between D/s and M/s structures—whether or not you agree with me:

While a *Dominant* has a strong *influence* over their submissive, I would argue that a Master has absolute authority over slave.

- A submissive gives limited control over certain aspects of their lives to their Dominant but retains enough personal autonomy that they may say "no" to a request from their Dom/me that they simply don't want to perform. While a decision based upon their own will would upset and annoy the Dom/me, it would seldom be viewed as relationship-ending.
- To become a slave, a person gives authority over themselves to their Master who now controls every aspect of their lives. For many, this person is now considered *owned property.*

A person does this for a variety of personal reasons that are hard to generalize. In this setting, slave's refusal to carry out an order that is within their power to fulfill would be seen as a willful act of disobedience and may well be taken by Master as a breach of the relationship's foundation: slave is to serve and to obey. Willful disobedience could easily be grounds for the slave's dismissal.

In my reality, the *ownership* issue separates Dominant/submissive (D/s) structures from Master/slave (M/s) structures.

Another distinction that I make, and will expand throughout this book, is that *Dominant* and *submissive* describe aspects of one's **personality** while *Master, Owner, slave*, and *property* describe **roles.** While it's unlikely that someone with a submissive personality would agree to take on the responsibility to master someone, that's a personal choice, not some kinky rule. While uncommon, one occasionally hears of a Master/slave structure where Master has instructed the slave to take on their own slave in order to better serve the Master. I lived that way for eight of the ten years that I was owned (before my current relationship). I know of other, similar situations.

There really is no rulebook. The best that I can do in this book is to get you to do some creative thinking.

"i believe that Masters and slaves are people who are willing to commit themselves to living in a way that is radically different from what our society teaches is right and appropriate. As people who choose to live in consensual Master/slave relationships, we defy some of the beliefs our society holds most dear: the belief that independence is the key to happiness and that the desire to control another person is the heart of abuse. It takes tremendous commitment to follow a path that at best is likely to be misunderstood by those around you."

—slave marsha, Keynote address, *Southwest Leather Conference*, December 5, 2003

Actually, that's a good way to think about this book: this book is about exploring sane, creative ways of forming a solid relationship that is *different* than a conventional boyfriend/girlfriend or husband/wife structure. It is also different from most D/s structures. But we'll get into that a bit further on in the book.

I've had some experience with being *misunderstood* as slave marsha puts it, particularly when I've tried to explain to vanillas (people who are not part of the overall BDSM community) why I choose to live in the world of authority-imbalanced relationships. Many people find it easier to avoid engaging me (and how I think) and simply dismiss me as nuts. This happens enough for me to notice it. It's as though it's easier to assume that I'm somehow broken as opposed to different.

Note: this book is a total rewrite/updating/expansion of my book, *Master/slave Relations: Handbook of theory and practice* (Nazca Plains, 2006) that almost since its publication became one of the foundation readings for people exploring D/s and M/s relations. However, times have changed and I have gained additional insights after twelve years of living on both sides of the slash in 24/7 M/s structures. Also, there are many more books/resources available now than when I wrote the previous book, and since that book came out, I have conducted hundreds of workshops on Master/slave topics all over the world. From the give-and-take that occurs during conference workshops, I've received quite a bit of feedback and additional perspectives. I've also gained insights and understanding as a result of having lived with my partner (and this book's co-author), Jen Fairfiled, since May 2011. Jen's idea of M/s (particularly her leadership style) was vastly different than mine. Because my own viewpoint has broadened, I decided to revise this book to make it more current.

So… Why have you bought this book?

Chances are, you bought this book because you fit into one of these four categories:

- You have formed or want to form a structured relationship. Your relationship may be a bit more D/s than M/s at this time, but you're interested in considering your options.

- You are an established Master or slave and you are curious about what someone could possibly write on the subject you think you know so well.

- You are finding yourself *called* to structure in a relationship but you're not sure what that means and you want to learn more about it before getting in over your head.

- You simply are curious about the M/s Lifestyle and are looking for in-depth information.

When you start exploring Master/slave (M/s) relationships, you start discovering a few truths. First, they are usually considered extremely radical/unusual. Second, they are often held up as the be-all and end-all of BDSM relationship structures. Third, you hear that they usually don't last very long.

Let me land on that last point for a moment. Have you ever wondered why so few Master/slave relationships last a long time? While living in (and studying, and writing, and lecturing about) structured relationships for over a decade, I've learned a thing or two about what helps and what hinders them. And that's what this book is about.

Without further fuss, here are my conclusions, but it will take the rest of this book to spread out the breadcrumbs that will lead you to these conclusions on your own.
- Know what you're getting into.
  - o Do you both agree on common terms and roles?
  - o Do you share a common understanding of *your version* of the elements of a structured relationship?
  - o Do you know when to stay in the relationship and work on it and when to stop the relationship and leave?
- Know what you need—as opposed to what you want: look inward.
  - o *Needs* are driven by your core values;
  - o *Wants* are generated when your personal list of successful and fun activities are combined with your imagination and fed by your ability to spend time, money, and energy to fulfill those *wants* in real time.

- Understand projections, dreams, and motivations. Are your/their expectations realistic?
  - Why do they want you? (Because you can give them emotional and financial security?)
  - Why do you want them? (Matching reason, or something quite different, such as a sex partner?)
- Know how to teach and how to learn.
  - Successful teachers know and apply a variety of teaching styles so their students can understand and apply their wisdom.
  - To successfully train or master another adult, you'll need to know how to move new ideas and behaviors through the subconscious *filters* and *psychological barriers* of another adult.
  - It's much easier to teach someone when they can start out by telling you how they learn.
- Know how to lead and how to follow.
  - Modern management theory describes the success/failure of various leadership approaches. Masters will benefit from knowing about the different styles as they related to their slaves: slaves will benefit from knowing about the different management styles as they work to fulfill Master's will.
  - The "Because I said so" approach is run by bullies; the "Because it's right for us" approach is run by leaders.
- Monitor relationship status.
  - Use protocols constantly and consistently to reaffirm/reinforce your respective roles.
  - Provide good service; acknowledge good service
  - Affirm your relationship; celebrate successes

This is a nice way to begin this book, for it presents a good overview. No, the book won't directly follow this outline: these are overall conclusions from the book.

I hope you enjoy the read.

In my experience…

I have found that couples who are living in Master/slave structures put a lot of work into it. In a way, they are relationship geeks. Particularly in the Leather form of M/s (a topic I'll take up in detail later in this book) terms such as *mindfulness*, *purpose*, and *intent* come up often.

In keeping with the kind of probing common to structured relationships, let me ask you some threshold questions: First, *why* do you want a Master or a slave? What is driving your *intention*? What do you *want* from a Master or a slave; why do you want this? What is it that a structured relationship can give you that you can't get from the land of vanillas? Second, what is your *purpose* in reading this book? Are you looking for an answer to some question, a key to some puzzle? If so, can you name what you're looking for? I only ask so you will know it when you find it—if you find it.

This is purely my own opinion, of course, but I think that structured relationships are VERY appealing for a variety of reasons:
- They encourage *mindful ways of thinking and behaving*. You're now in a relationship in which you and your partner are both concerned about such concepts as *purpose, intent,* and *mindfulness.*
- Often, structured relationships enable us to uncover things about ourselves. It's about self-actualization; about confronting what is next for us and working through our own psychological blocks.
- These relationships bring out the best (and worst) in people. You'll have the time of your life if you're an empathetic and farsighted leader: if you're not so gifted, you have the opportunity of a lifetime to change yourself to be happier in your own skin.
- Structured relationships take a god-awful amount of work. At some point you're likely to find yourself wondering whether it's all worth it. It is at this point that Master must honestly assess whether or not he/she is willing to *pay the price* to re-energize the relationship so it operates as it was initially designed. For many, this is the point at which Master confronts

a key question: is it in the slave's best interest to *sustain the illusion* that the relationship, itself, is functional. I'll cover the concept of *sustaining the illusion* in greater depth in *Master/ slave Mastery: refining the fire-ideas that matter* (Book Two in the Master/slave Mastery Series)
- They're *traditional*. They're essentially consensual marriage structures from a more formal era.

My approach to this (or any new) field can be summarized in a phrase: "When you don't know what to do, do it slowly" (Jim Hayhurst, Sr.). Not only do it slowly, but also do it *thoroughly* lest you get surprised in unpleasantly complicated ways. This book contains a lot of detail; some sections assume that you are pretty well advanced in the BDSM Lifestyle. Let me mention at the outset that I strongly recommend that you read six books as companions to this book. In my opinion, these are the classics—the foundation reading for those interested in learning about authority-based relationships.
- Guy Baldwin, *Slavecraft*. Daedalus Publishing Company, 2002.
- Guy Baldwin, *Ties that Bind*. Daedalus Publishing Company,
- 1993.
- Larry Townsend, *Leatherman's Handbook*. L.T. Publications,
- 2000.
- Jack Rinella, *Becoming a Slave*. Rinella's Editorial Services,
- 2005.
- Joushua Tenpenny and Raven Kladera *Real Service*. Alfred
- Press, 2011
- david stein (Ed) *Ask the Man Who Owns Him: The real lives of gay Masters and slaves*. Perfect Bound Press, 2009

Let's start with the question: What are **you** looking for?
- An occasional slave for play or a permanent slave?
- A slave who takes independent action on behalf of the Master, or a slave who is essentially in neutral (called *attending*) when not engaged in a specific task assigned by the Master.
- A structured relationship with protocols (think *baking a cake*) or an amorphous one (think *making a stew*)? [Note: Sergeant Major (Fet = TheSergeantMajor) shared the *cake* vs. *stew* analogy with me in about 2010 and subsequently used it in

some of his presentations. We had been discussing differences between our slave-management styles.]

- A monogamous relationship or a polyamorous set of relationships? If poly, are you thinking of including other slaves?
- Is your life to be centered on sadomasochism (SM—pleasure or pain associated with giving or receiving intense experiences sometimes including pain) or something else?

And—once you have some ideas of what you ARE looking for, what kind of *structure* might best support that goal?

At the risk of complicating the discussion...

As I write this 2014 revision to my 2006 initial manuscript I'd like to challenge you to a concept that I've been considering for about a year: Where one falls on the scale of dominance and submission concerns how one acts/behaves as a leader or follower. While the degree of one's dominance or submission has everything to do with a D/s dynamic, I'm not so sure that it's very important in an M/s dynamic. That is, I'm growing in the conviction that slavery is about service, not about submission. Yes, the slave has to submit to the will of Master, but terms such as *subordinate/subordination* also come to mind. In Military parlance, one doesn't advance through the officer ranks by being submissive to one's superiors; one advances through the ranks by performing superior service. I'll argue the same point here: While *submission* is the defining characteristics in a D/s structure, in an M/s structure, the defining characteristics include **purposeful intent, obedience,** and *service*. This helps explain the existence of the ubiquitous *alpha slave* or *dominant slave* that Master Skip Chasey noted as one of the hallmarks of a gay Leather slave (See Master Skip's article included in the book *Ask the Man who Owns Him* compiled by david stein).

What are structured relationships?

"Structured relationships," (also called *power-exchange relationships* or *authority-based relationships or authority-imbalanced relationships*) include about any way of working together that is not power-equal: these forms of relationships are structurally different than vanilla boyfriend/girlfriend or husband/wife.

It's been my experience that structured relationships come in two flavors:
- Power-imbalanced relationships (often referred to as D/s)
- Authority-imbalanced relationships (often referred to as M/s for Master/slave, O/p for Owner/property, or TPE for Total Power Exchange)

Some background

Dominant and *submissive* are also personality descriptors, not only role descriptors. Master and slave are role descriptors, not personality descriptors. Not meaning to speak shorthand, but D/s and M/s represent relationship tags that have substantially different meanings…

It is one thing to play Master and slave in a scene and it's another thing to have a part-time M/s relationship. However, it is quite different to live 24/7 with someone where you are either Master (with total authority over—and responsibility for—another) or as slave (where you have surrendered personal authority over your time and give up the right to say "no" to your Master).

By the way, in that last paragraph it may take a keen reader to catch that I said that Master has *authority* over their slave. In this level of relationship, Master is not said to have *control* over slave, but to have authority over slave. Big difference. One has control over one's car, but it doesn't help you avoid accidents. Authority over someone is quite a responsibility.

The world of Master/slave is very roughly divided into two schools of thought—Leather and not-Leather. Not-Leather is called BDSM by those of us in Leather.

Actually, whether Master is leading with *authority* or with *control* turns out to be one of the key factors that affect the way Master structures the relationship, for authority-based management is *outward looking*, control-based management is *inward looking*. People in authority are looking outside their relationship, scanning their horizon to be sure that they are (figuratively) in the right place and performing the correct action with those under their care. People in control are looking inside their relationship to be sure that their subordinates are following orders.

You'll find other startling differences in relationship management styles once you start teasing apart personality traits. As an example, consider the *towards vs. away from* personality traits that are described in Neuro-Linguistic Programming (NLP) instruction. Some people work *towards* something while other people live their lives to stay *away from* something. Think of entrepreneurial drive versus the motivations of a CPA or defense attorney. One is pulled *towards* newness and excitement; the other is trained to keep clients *away from* trouble.

Applying this *toward/away from* perspective to an M/s relationship, one can imagine that some slaves have entered the relationship to support someone they admired and from whom they could learn (*toward* behavior) while others have surrendered authority over themselves in order to be cared for and guided in life (*away from* behavior—in this case, away from personal responsibility over themselves).

Distinctions such as these should become second nature to you by the time you finish this book.

Dominant/submissive (D/s) relationships
From the outset, let me draw a distinction that Midori makes that there are two different arenas in which Dominance and submission play out: one is sexual D/s and the other is relationship D/s. Translation: D/s bedroom scenes may or may not involve psychological D/s outside the bedroom and psychological D/s structures may or may not involve sex.

Sexual D/s focuses on surrender and control of sexual power and erotic behavior—within a prescribed time period. Relational D/s focuses on the authority imbalance aspect of your lives together. You may be in a part-time D/s relationship—only when interacting together—or in a full-time (24/7) D/s relationship.

D/s relationships involve *power exchange*. Unless you're actually living in a D/s relationship, you'll most likely run into this form of power exchange when you are engaged in a BDSM play scene. In that case, D/s play is situational and time-limited. D/s play negotiations involve discussions of likes, dislikes, limits, and medical/psychological concerns.

For some, D/s is about micromanagement. The submissive is not supposed to do anything that the Dom/me doesn't direct. Master Skip Chasey refers to D/s play as being about the *mental body*. Master Steve Sampson looks at this play as being about *energy*.

Despite the BDSM sense that D/s **play** is time-limited, one also sees long-lasting relationships that have grown to incorporate **negotiated D/s** into a marriage or marriage-like relationship. In fact, many see power exchange relationships as an effective way that two people can choose well-defined roles for themselves and their partner(s). There is a dominant partner who has leadership responsibility and there is a submissive partner whose responsibilities include both preserving harmony and supporting the dominant. The two (or more) work out ways that their individual abilities can best meet their common needs.

A D/s relationship differs from a vanilla relationship in a number of ways—at least in theory:

D/s relationships, roles are carefully pre-negotiated rather than assumed based on gender. For example, within most traditional marriages, the man takes over the financial and relationship-vision roles, while the woman assumes responsibility for the house and kids. It just happens; the roles are culturally driven, not assigned after thoughtful deliberation.

There is generally more accountability in D/s relationships than in traditional marriages. In most marriages, if the husband is displeased with the way his wife has done something, he's likely either to ignore it as too inconsequential to address or point out the deficiency—but take no further action (frankly, he's likely simply to finish the job the way he wanted and be done with it). From the woman's point of view, when the man acts in a way that she believes to be socially inappropriate or is limiting her in ways she does not like, she is likely to test her authority to change her spouse's behavior a time or two and/or conclude that it is not within her role as dutiful wife to comment/intervene in the way her husband behaves.

On the other side of this coin, though—in a D/s structure where personal accountability is an active part of the relationship—the Dom is *very likely* to hold the submissive accountable for their actions and will correct (or even punish) the submissive when a task is not done correctly. Conversely, a Dom must exhibit above-average ethical and leadership behaviors so the submissive will continue (voluntarily) to serve.

The submissive partner's needs are more likely to be met in a D/s relationship than in most traditional marriages. No, I can't prove it, but I strongly suspect that to be true. I believe this happens because of the emphasis on negotiations, communication, and ethical/responsible behavior—and because of ongoing discussions about wants/needs and roles/responsibilities. Said differently, less is assumed because both partners are exploring an unusual relationship structure—so they talk about it.

Partners tend to be more *present* in healthy D/s relationships than in traditional vanilla relationships as a by-product of the mutual acknowledgement and relationship maintenance that must go on: partners in these kinds of intentional relationship structures are less inclined to take one another for granted.

Master/slave (M/s) relationships

Note: Before saying *anything* about M/s structures readers must understand that the M/s relationship is about *roles* much more than it is about dominance and submission. *Master* is the Family's visionary leader, responsible for establishing and maintaining the Family's purpose. Where the Master or slave falls on the dominant/submissive scale of personality characteristics takes a back seat to the Master's leadership abilities and the slave's dedication to serving Master's vision through perfect obedience.

At this level, couples themselves establish the specific rules and practices that work for them. The M/s dynamic is generally considered the most far-reaching form of BDSM-related relationship. In this form of relationship, slave has given Master complete authority over itself.

Many M/s relationships begin with a contract that includes paragraphs describing the scope and limits of the M/s dynamic. But that very act, the act of the potential Master and slave working together to hammer out a negotiated agreement by which Master will operate the M/s dynamic, is viewed by some as something less than a total commitment to the concept of M/s where slave has no authority over itself. This has given rise to a new relationship category—Owner/slave—discussed in the next section.

Now: a caveat. What I'm about to write is true in my experience and may not be true in the experience of others with whom you speak about Masters and slaves. There simply is no rulebook about those who follow this Path.

In my experience, the M/s dynamic differs from the D/s dynamic in a number of key ways.

- First, for all practical matters, Master has total authority over the slave—as compared with the Dom/me's authority that may be restricted in certain negotiated areas (most often in areas involving the slave's biological family, work, religion, etc.).

- Second, Master is 100% responsible for all aspects of the slave's wellbeing—mental health, physical health, finances, education, training, etc.

- Third, in part due to their complexity (and in part due to the customs established decades ago within the gay Leather community) M/s structures often involve a written contract that defines the terms of the *offer* and *acceptance* and they also often involve a written code of personal and household protocols that describe the way the slave is to behave and the way the household is to run.

- Fourth, the slave in an M/s relationship is really an extension of the Master's/Owner's will; an *advance-man* or *personal assistant*. In that capacity, the slave is expected to know how to react as Master would, and to prepare any setting to conform to Master's wishes.

This point is actually very, very important: unlike a vanilla relationship where two autonomous people trying to make their way in the world as a couple, in a structured M/s relationship, one of slave's responsibilities is to know and to fulfill Master's wants/needs. This aspect of the relationship will come up later in this book, because it can be a tripping-point unless Master knows how to use the additional knowledge that slave has acquired about Master.

- Fifth, Master usually establishes specific *protocols* (ways of doing things) for slave to follow. As the slave learns the way Master wants things done (learns Master's protocols), the slave becomes able to anticipate and move to meet Master's unspoken needs. This is sometimes referred to as *anticipatory service*. Under Master's guidance, the couple is increasingly blended into one being that expresses what we might call "Master's World Outlook." Often, the M/s dynamic involves spiritual growth that is not common to relationships involving other power dynamics. Both Master Skip and Master Steve consider Master/slave relationships to be about the spiritual body. I know of a number of long-term marriages that incorporate an M/s structure, though these are quite rare: it is often difficult to change years of equal-partner marriage into a stable authority-imbalanced structure.
Writing down Master's expectations of the slave's roles in the relationship helps to remove petty annoyances and irritations. Also, writing down the slave's expected behaviors in common situations enables Master to focus on larger tasks/challenges without having to be concerned about what slave is doing. As a side benefit, the slave now clearly knows what is expected in virtually all situations and does not have to think about (or

"…people who know and follow the path of Mastery or slavery are called. They believe they were **called** to follow a different path than the ones our society prescribes for us."

—slave marsha, Keynote address, Southwest Leather Conference: December 5, 2003.

worry about) whether or not he/she is meeting Masters needs. (Readers are referred to books on *protocols* listed in the Supplements).

As you learn more about M/s structures, you will learn that unlike the popularized version in which the slave's primary reason-for-being is to satisfy Master's wants, this can be a very, very sophisticated structure in which the Master is serving the slave's needs every bit as much as the slave is endeavoring to fulfill Master's wants. You will increasingly hear the phrase: "While the slave serves Master, Master serves the relationship."

For many of us who use the M/s dynamic for spiritual connection, the greatest challenge for the slave is what is called *ego surrender*. Rather than go into that here, I recommend you to Joshua Tenpenny and Raven Kaldea's book *Sacred Power* for more on this topic. Please refer to the Supplements for resources to help you further explore this area. This is advanced material and not appropriate for this book.

About dancing and learning

This may be a stretch for some of you, but here goes. You'll have to cooperate, here, or this isn't going to *click* for you.

In your mind, I want you to think back on all the kinky people you know who are in relationships of some kind. D/s, Daddy/girl, M/s, Owner/property… you name it. All these couples are lined up in your mind. They're all about to go out onto a dance floor—let's say a Country-Western dance floor. The music starts and out they all go. The floor is fairly crowded, but nobody is bumping into anyone—they all have room to do their own thing.

Those of you who have gone dancing on a Friday night realize that most people on the dance floor are trying to wing it. They haven't taken lessons; they don't want to take lessons. Lessons aren't necessary: after all, how hard can it be to dance to music. *Dancing*, according to them, is about fun and lessons aren't *fun*. Besides, they're naturals—they haven't needed to take lessons in the past in order to dance.

But, then you see a few couples that have clearly had some lessons. They're better; their movements are more interesting than most of the dancers and the couples are working together to accomplish a common goal—to dance. You're enjoying the show along with your beer. Then the music picks up in tempo and the weaker dancers leave the floor: now most of the couples that are left seem to know what they're doing: the turns and patterns they are dancing are substantially more complex than those of the dancers who have now left the floor. And a few of the couples are magnificent. One couple dances by and something causes you to watch them. They are fascinating; what they are doing is magical. You can't take your eyes off of them. The leader is giving seemingly invisible signals that the follower seems to understand intuitively. They are going through dance moves and patterns you've only seen on TV. Because you, yourself, know something about dancing, you notice that on beat 6 (the second *slow* of the Country-Western dance pattern that is called out as *quick-quick-slow-slow*) the couple is accentuating whatever pattern they're in AND they are *dancing to the music* (rather than: *there is music playing and they are dancing*). This is seriously sophisticated shit. The gulf between your level of dance knowledge and their level of dance knowledge seems unbridgeable.

That's the way it is with those of us who live successfully in Master/slave relationships: they're cerebral; they require work; they do not succeed by accident.

You don't join the Army as a General; you don't step off the street and onto a dance floor as a regional competitor; you don't go directly from boyfriend/girlfriend to M/s. It doesn't work that way.

A word of caution...

This is a book mostly about working with relationships based on *authority transfer*. Authority transfer is the term that I prefer to use to describe the condition wherein one person transfers their authority over him/herself to make decisions about what they do *on their own initiative* (such as going out to check the mail) for the partner's agreement to take responsibility for their total wellbeing—educational, medical, spiritual, social, intellectual and financial.

If you are searching for a book that deals with the internal operations of a relationship based on more temporary (and limited) *power exchange*, I'm not sure this is your book. Furthermore, if your experience with *power exchange* comes from the Internet—if you have not actually had a *power exchange relationship* before—this book probably needs to rest in your bookcase until you've built some real-life experience. Before you venture into the world of M/s relationships, you may first wish to spend some time learning how to manage a D/s relationship. Also, real-life M/s unions feel very different from long-distance or Internet relationships—even though they may seem to be based upon M/s theory. I know, this is a personal assertion and not a fact; I'd be interested to hear from anyone whose experience is different.

Chapter 2
Common Understandings

"In M/s, we explore with intent," says my friend Bob Ritchie (Fet=Bydarra). So very true. M/s is a very cerebral form of relationship structure. I've written this section to be sure that we're all meaning the same things by the words we use.

First, this material is NOT completely generalizable. In the same way that no two marriages are completely alike, no two approaches to living as a Master/slave couple are completely alike. However, while there are many ways to approach these *structured relationships*, the experiences of those who have gone before—those who actively live this lifestyle—can be instructive.

So, let's start out by using some definitions get ourselves on the same page. You don't have to agree with these, just consider them to be *operational definitions* for the purpose of making it through this book; as there are regional differences in Leather protocols, so there are regional differences in the meanings of some terms used in our subculture.

This alphabetized list is intended only to express how I am using these words throughout this book. I make no assertion that others will agree with definitions; we just have to settle on *some* definitions of these words.

Also, when it comes to terms such as Dominant and submissive, keep in mind that these are attributes that live on a sliding scale that—itself—is contextual. That is, no matter how dominant you are at home or at work, you're just not very likely to express that level of dominance should you find yourself sitting before some kind of criminal justice investigatory body—regardless of who you are. No matter how submissive you are at home or at work, you're just not very likely to express that level of submissiveness should you find yourself needing to defend your child or mate.

Words and the way I use them

Dom or Domme
A dominant is a person who takes control during specific (often negotiated) periods. That is why D/s relationships are often associated with BDSM (Bondage, Discipline, Sado-masochism) scening (a scene is an encounter that may or may not include sexual activity. It can take place in private or in a public BDSM party or club.)

Master (adj)
A term often applied to a Leatherman who has earned such respect within the Community that other senior Leathermen refer to this person as Master (regardless of gender). This respect is generally granted after years of selfless contribution to the Leather Community as a whole.

Master (n)
A man or woman who exerts near total control over another—often pursuant to a negotiated contract. The issue, here, is whether the person plays primarily in the world of *authority transfer* rather than in the world of *power exchange*. For our purposes, a Master takes authority over another either for a contracted period or permanently (more on this at a later point). A Master is a Dominant who could occasionally bottom to someone, even his own slave who is now *serving Master* through the action of Topping. In this sense, the Master is referred to as versatile. The Master's primary responsibility is to do everything within their power to maximize the potential of their slave(s). This involves such things as:

- Maintaining and protecting the trust given to him/her by the slave's submission.

- Being clear about the terms and conditions of the slave's service, including restrictions on the slave's activities and Master's rights to use the slave.
- Ensuring the slave's physical, social, emotional, spiritual, and financial wellbeing.
- Providing whatever training, direction and guidance is necessary to develop the slave to their true potential.
- Establishing and maintaining effective lines of communication with the slave.
- Exercising care and sound judgment in the relationship, as the slave's condition and conduct reflects upon the Master and their House.

One current hot topic concerns whether or not a person can be a Master unless he or she has a slave—someone who actually *calls* the person *Master*. The eloquent answer to this question comes from Master JW: "A magnet is still a magnet whether it's in the presence of metal or not. If your relationship needs are met by being responsible for and in control of another person and you consider yourself to be a leader of people when participating in this way of life, then whether or not you happen to have a slave at the time does not affect the authenticity of your mastery."

"Obviously," Master JW adds, "the obverse is also true: You don't need to have a Master to live authentically as a slave—either in service to mankind or simply waiting until you find a suitable Master."

Owner
As I previously said, the term *Owner* is starting to be used to describe a permanent M/s relationship based on a simple exchange of profound vows. The Owner pledges to take care of all of the slave's needs and the slave pledges to obey and to serve their Owner. Period. Permanently. No contract.

Protocols
In the military sense, protocols are a directed series of steps to be followed in a given situation to create a defined, reproducible result. Protocols are used to create an effective *governance structure* in an M/s relationship.

Rituals

Rituals set the tone for something that is about to happen or is happening. Rituals are a preferred way doing something. For example, you may have a ritual of having cocktails before dinner in your living room while there is a fire burning in the fireplace. Within that ritual, you may have a dozen protocols that concern who sets the fireplace, how the appetizers and cocktails are prepared and served, and how the lights, candles, and music are all set up.

You get into **ritual** through **theatrics** that involve as many of the senses as you can.

Submissive and slave

First, some prefatory notes: I'll begin by proposing that *submissive* and *slave* motivations and behaviors aren't quite the same. While one is certainly not better than the other, one set of behaviors is more likely to fit some people than others. At the most fundamental level, one speaks about *having* a submissive versus *owning* a slave. That, itself, is a window into the profound differences between the two.

Although the descriptions that I'm about to provide sound neat and clean, it's not that way in real life. Some people dislike one or another word (Master, slave, etc) and perform those behaviors while calling themselves by a word that seems less harsh to them. For example, some s-types identify as *submissives* even though they have surrendered authority over themselves to their Dom/me. While they refer to themselves as *submissives*, their relationship structure appears objectively to be closer to *slave* than to *sub*. Similarly, the Dom/mes in control of such s-types do not consistently refer to themselves as Master. This rich complexity of relationship structures and roles—this land of flexibility and possibility—makes the BDSM world hard to understand yet lots of fun to live in.

Here is my version of a graduate-school level synopsis of this discussion: *Dominant* and *submissive* describe aspects of one's personality; *slave* or *property* describes roles one can assume whether one has a dominant or submissive personality. The *slave* or *property* roles have to do with *slaveheart* or service—and your choice about how you wish to behave around a particular person/partner. This gets confusing, because *to have a submissive personality* gets mixed up with the role of *being the subordinate partner*. There are certainly cases where a self-identified dominant has chosen to be the subordinate partner in a relationship. *That does not make them a submissive person.* In the terminology of Chris M. Lyon this makes them the *supportive* (as opposed to *submissive*) partner. Chris M. Lyon is the author of the fabulously insightful book: *Leading and Supportive Love: the Truth About Dominant and Submissive Relationships.*)

In my world, the *behaviors* and *actions* of a person filling the *submissive* role in a D/s structure can be almost indistinguishable from a person filling the *slave* role in an M/s structure. The key issues: First, while the submissive has the authority to negotiate areas where they retain personal authority and control, the slave does not; second, D/s structures tend to have far fewer and less formal protocols than M/s structures; third, unlike D/s structures, M/s structures tend to start out with contracts between the two parties. With some trepidation, I'll add a fourth key issue that exists more in the Leather world than in the BDSM world: a *Master* must be a good leader but may or may not have a very dominant personality while a dominant in a D/s relationship is clearly a person with a *dominant* personality—and may or may not be a good leader (they may be more of a bully than a true leader—leading by fear rather than by inspiration).

Submissives and slaves are individuals, and individuals differ in countless ways. Each relationship is different and our conduct within each relationship is different. Whether one considers oneself to be a *submissive*, a *slave*, or *property* is partly a matter of personal choice and partly a matter of loosely observed definitions.

All that being said, here is how I define the two roles…

submissive: A person who chooses at certain times and within certain conditions to submit to the will of their partner. The conditions typically including terms of service, length of service, areas of the submissives' life the dominant does not get to control, the hard and soft limits when they play or just interact, and the safewords they will use when scening. Although it is counterintuitive, the submissive has some degree of

23

control over an SM play scene through safewords—at least until they enter subspace.

Some typical characteristics of the submissive's role:
- D/s relationship is based on power *exchange*. (This means that the submissive—a person who normally has as much or as little personal control as society gives them—will now surrender some of that personal control to the Dom/me for a prescribed period in exchange for specific benefits negotiated from the D-type.)
- Submissives have a strong desire to serve—but that service is limited to their Dom/me and is offered with certain negotiated conditions.
- Typically, the negotiated area include the submissive's terms of service, the length of that service, the hard and soft limits, and the safewords.
- The submissive will also negotiate those aspects of their life that the Dom doesn't control. These aspects often include the submissive's biological family and children, work, education and religious observance.
- The conditions under which the submissive is willing to serve can be renegotiated (This is a major issue: the submissive retains the personal authority to ask their Dominant to renegotiate their terms of service, but the Dominant is under no obligation to accept the newly proposed conditions.)
- If the Dom breaks the submissives hard limits, the scene would end and—in the case of a breach of a relationship trust—the relationship could end.
- The Dom may be permitted to break *soft limits* (things the submissive has said they really aren't interested in) after discussing it with the submissive and obtaining their permission.
- In many/most cases, submissives cross back and forth between retaining and surrendering control over some aspect of their lives and continue to make decisions in the areas that are off-limits for their Dom
- A submissive re-submits to the Dom at the start of any scene or activity over which the Dom has negotiated authority. Importantly, the submissive retains the choice as to whether or not to submit to the Dom.

slave: A person who has transferred authority over him/herself to another. In a general sense, the distinction between a *submissive* and *slave* focuses on whether the person retains any personal authority and/or retains any meaningful decision-making capabilities or surrenders such authority to someone else. Also, play rules are usually different for slaves, as they lack the authority to tell their Master to stop a scene.

Some typical characteristics of a consensual slave's role:
- M/s relationship is based on authority *transfer.* (This means that once the person who is to become the slave has, in fact, surrendered personal authority over him/herself to their Master/Owner, they no longer have the personal power to make decisions for him/herself. Thus, a slave would not have the authority to enter into a D/s scene with someone other than their Master/Owner without that Master/Owner's specifically transferring THEIR authority over their own slave to another person. Likewise, if their Master/Owner tells them to participate in a scene with someone else, they are expected to comply.)
- At least in theory, the slave gives up all rights to make personal decisions and becomes the *property* of a Master or Owner.
- The core values are *service* and *obedience.*
- The slave loses the right to say "no" to Master: in its place, slave may say, "Sir, if it pleases you, Sir" to mean: "Master, I really rather would not do that." or "Sir, only if it pleases you, Sir" which is as close to "no" as slave is permitted. (Note: Master has an ethical obligation only to push through an *only if* reply so long as Master thinks that doing so remains in the slave's best interest. Requiring a slave to proceed through an *only if* command on Master's whim violates the basic Master/slave pact on Master's part and represents a contract violation.)
- As slave cannot *red out* (stop the scene using a safeword), slave thus has accepted their Master's limits and does what is asked of them regardless of their feelings about it. (*What does liking it have to do with it?*)
- A slave will have no rights to personal property and will continue to work for the benefit of Master's household or business.

- A slave's purpose is to make Master's life easier. In that regard, a slave is expected to know Master's wants and likes to the extent that the slave can take independent action on Master's behalf (proactive rather than reactive; to show initiative as a thinking person)
- An act of willfulness can terminate a relationship. This is particularly true in cases where a slave removes their own collar or actually says "no" to a direct order. Master cannot function if command authority is questioned. (In the Military model, the parallel would be Court Marshall pursuant to disobeying a direct order.)
- May be more interested in taking care of others (service heart) than in being taken care of (*sorts by others* vs. *sorts by self* in psychology-speak).
- May very well be a dominant in most other aspects of their life, but have chosen to be submissive to (or simply to serve) one single person

Okay, now that we have gone over the terms themselves, I want to demonstrate what happens when you combine them into relationship structures.

D/s and M/s

I want to start out by proposing an entirely different way of thinking about D/s and M/s.

After thinking about structured relationships for years and after speaking with countless people about this topic, I now propose that D/s and M/s discussions are not even related. I propose that D/s is a conversation about personality—how dominant or submissive one is—and that M/s is a conversation about roles—whether you are leading or following.

In my experience, M/s concerns roles people take within a structured relationship that focuses upon:
- authority;
- responsibility of command; and
- depth and scope of command.

Living D/s—to me—really says:
- we are two kinky people living together in love;
- one of us has some negotiated degree of control over the other;
- SM is the common bond; and
- sex is part of the package.

Living M/s—to me—really says:
- one person is in command of, and has authority over, the other person;
- the subordinate person has pledged to serve and obey the person in charge;
- whether or not love is involved is a matter of interpersonal chemistry and is not a de facto component of the relationship. (The Captain does not have to love his Colonel to follow the Colonel's orders.);
- where the subordinate person falls on the dominant-submissive scale has nothing to do with serving in the position either of Master or of slave;
- SM play may or may not have anything to do with the relationship; and
- sex may or may not have anything to do with the relationship.

As my friend Brett (Fet = LTR) points out, "Whether you settle on a relationship that is D/s, M/s, Owner/property, or Daddy/girl, all structures have in common that they demonstrate that the s-type is cared for, supervised, and monitored. Terms like *Master, Daddy,* and *Sir* are the s-types idiom of affection."

Two approaches to M/s

Leatherfolk use the term "BDSM" to describe what kinky straight folk do; they do **not** use the term "BDSM" to describe what *they* do. They describe what *they* do as "rough trade" or "rough sex." It can be confusing to try to discuss these two aspects of the world of alternate sexuality. That's why I use the terms *Leather* and *not-Leather* rather than *Leather* and *BDSM*.

When you listen to senior members of the Leather and not-Leather communities describe what it is that we do, it comes down to this: **Leather** is really a euphemism for *gay men having kinky sex,* and **BDSM** is really a euphemism that means *heterosexual people having kinky sex.* That much is pretty easy to derive.

The thing of it is, while the participants in these two groups are *appearing* to do very similar things (such as flogging someone), the activity often *looks* quite different when you're standing right there watching it happening. Over the years of doing just that—watching—I have finally concluded that the difference concerns the Leathermen's application of *intent and purpose* as they use their tools to *work* with their bottom. This difference is actually so profound that it's hard to put into words. It's as though the straight BDSM crowd who uses toys for play sessions have learned techniques without learning why one applies them. When you go to most BDSM play parties, if you're seeing a flogging, you're seeing a flogging. However, if you step into a male-only play space at a Leather conference and see a flogging, you'll recognize that you're looking at something quite different.

I've been challenged to explain that difference. After observing play at a lot of conferences, it is my experience that flogging scenes in a Leather dungeon are riveting—it is obvious that something *special* is going on. Flogging scenes in a BDSM play space are frequently fun to watch, but it is my personal sense is that there is something missing. Perhaps it is the psychological aspect, perhaps it has something to do with the *intent of the scene.* Perhaps it's that the intent is to have a flogging scene rather than an intent of something greater than a flogging scene. I can only share my sense that some BDSMers are missing an element in their scenes that is, in fact, understood among those practicing Leathersex.

Well—much the same can be said about how Master/slave structures work in the Leather and not-Leather (BDSM) worlds: they're are usually quite different.

- When **Leatherfolk** speak about their M/s relationships, you'll often hear them speak about protocols, obedience, spirituality, and service.

- When **BDSMers** speak about their M/s relationships, you often hear them speak about using humiliation as a training technique, breaking their slave, and punishment.

Because this divide is so philosophically important, many straights that have felt themselves called to Mastery and slavery have declared themselves also to be called to the Leather path. I'm one of those. While I recognize and agree with Master Skip Chasey's statement that you can't *really* be a Leatherman unless you are gay and an active participant in a gay Leather community, we nonetheless honor and respect the approach that many Leathermen have taken when forming their structured relationships. We'd rather be associated with concepts of spirituality, obedience, and service than with the practices of humiliating and psychologically breaking another human being. Perhaps Master Skip will permit us all to be Honorary Leathermen?

I'm stressing the differences between these two approaches because they carry implications in relation to how Masters and slaves get together and interact in this current age. These different paths affect the Master's and the slave's role expectations. While those following the Leather path are thinking such things as *high moral purpose, focus, service,* and *responsibility,* those on the not-Leather path are often thinking about such things as *unpaid maid service* and *sexual fantasy fulfillment*—often unconsciously and without having discussed role expectations with the intended slave.

And, there are other differences, sometimes quite subtle. We'll now explore a few of these.

The *BDSM* Path to M/s
The not-Leather M/s path bases much of their M/s practices on their personal interpretation of fictionalized versions of masters and slaves from novels, movies, TV shows, and books about cultures that actually had slaves. However, unlike the military values of service and obedience that became the core values of the gay Leather version of M/s, the heterosexual version of M/s starts out with a boy/girl couple who are exploring BDSM relationship options. That is, the BDSM version of Master/slave relationships is almost always based on amorous (albeit kinky) love: say hello to *Fifty Shades of Grey.*

While there are undoubtedly exceptions among heterosexuals who are following the BDSM rather than the Leather path, it's been my experience that Doms tend to be looking for submissives for play, and that over time, the D/s relationship transforms into a live-in relationship that later flows into an M/s relationship—often with little or no formality. In my experience, this type of metamorphosis is very uncommon in the Leather world where there is no parallel for a D/s structure. (No, Daddy/boy is nurture-based, not service-based: different deal.)

The *Leather* path to M/s

What we now refer to as the Leather culture had its roots in returned GIs from World War II who blended some features of their military experiences with their kinky interests as they banded together to form tight-knit communities necessary in the 1950s and 60s for self-protection. Some of the distant echoes of their quasi-military rules of protocol, inclusion, and exclusion can still be seen in today's Leather BDSM society.

While there are no absolutes, there is a *general tendency* in the Leather community for a slave who has come to know a particular Master for a long time to petition him to become his slave (or to join his Family). Also, there is a general tendency among Leather Masters to consider it their duty/obligation to accept such petitions as a *gift from the Universe* and to provide personal guidance to this person (to *master* them) so long as the Master deems that person ready and able to be mastered. In fact, this brings up another tradition within the Leather culture: sometimes when a Master takes on a new slave, part of the negotiations concern *intention*. Is it the slave's *intention* that he/she be developed into a full-time, permanent slave for that particular Master or is it the slave's intention that they are being mentored to become a Master in their own right after some period of training?

As I said a few paragraphs ago, to Leatherfolk, physical BDSM play is what kinky straight folk do. After studying the Leather and BDSM communities for over a decade, my strong impression is that physical BDSM play imitates the actions first taught by Leathermen (flogging, caning, eStim, etc), but without the Leatherman's understanding of the purpose or intent of the actions. It's like the difference between emotionally connected sex versus a casual fuck session.

When applying these distinctions to the world of M/s relationships, I'm not proposing that one approach is better than another. I'm only pointing out that there are two quite different starting points: an s-type petitioning to be a particular Master's slave because of that Master's known reputation strikes me as very different from a D-type person seeking a submissive and transitioning them into their version of a slave.

Oh, before I leave this section about differences between the Leather and BDSM approaches to M/s relationships, I'd like to add one more note. You may remember that in the first few pages of this book I explained that in my view, whether or not the person was said to be "owned" represented the dividing line between an owned slave and a voluntary submissive? Well, that comes up again here, as I believe that for many, the *intent* of M/s is that Master *owns* the slave, while for many who have D/s structures (particularly those where amorous love is central) the Dom/me wants to *possess* the submissive. In the latter instance, ownership does not carry an emotional connotation beyond words such as *pride* and *satisfaction*.

M/s as Way of Living

By and large, the earliest uses of *Master/slave* terminology referred to short-term role-play in consensual sex scenes. For example, in dark, smoky gay bars, a *boy* (bottom) might ask a Top to be his *Master* and take him home as his slave for the night to do whatever Master wanted to do to him. But this Master/slave role-play was conceived not as a long-term relationship but as a hot sexy scene for the night or weekend. The role-play wasn't intended to last.

Long-term M/s came later—and from the heterosexual world. The idea reached the popular imagination through *The Story of O* that first appeared in the English translation in 1955, and many books since have added to the concept, including the marvelous and extensive writings of Laura Antoniou in her *Marketplace* series.

While I understand that weekend M/s scening (and the public media fantasy image of Master/slave structures) features a Master who is never wrong and slave serving under totalitarian conditions for reasons known only to them, that's not the reality for any stable M/s relationship that I've ever heard of. The reality is that Master must be serving slave as much as slave is serving Master. To quote my eloquent friend Dan (Fet= DanielBelum) "Master is owned by the relationship; slave is owned by Master."

I know; heresy. Being slightly crass about it, the minute a wage-earning slave enters Master's Household, Master (at the very least) becomes dependent upon that slave in order to maintain the Household's new standard of living. Not only that, but to the extent that the slave makes Master's life easier, Master is dependent upon that slave for those services. If Master intends those services to continue, payback takes the form of Master providing total protection and support for the slave. That means acting consistently in slave's best interest and understanding and guarding areas that are slave's particular vulnerabilities. Translation: many people fear being abandoned or rejected; the slave's emotional stability depends upon Master's emotionally-supportive words and deeds.

Yes, slave is serving Master and yes, Master can set a high bar in terms of the slave's obedience. I believe that Raven Kaldera has captured the spirit of the slave's required mindset with his phrase *absolute commitment to Master's authority.* In my view, that says it all.

Examples of M/s relationship structures

There are so many combinations of ways to do things in the world of 24/7 M/s structures that no real categorization is possible. However, when one steps back from the trees to survey the forest, it's possible to discern certain schools of thought or grouping of behavioral characteristics.

As I say repeatedly in my presentations and in my writings, structured relationships are not generalizable. M/s structures are run so differently that it's hard to tease out the common characteristics.

And, it doesn't help that those of who live M/s use the same terms but attach somewhat different meanings to them. For example, *to serve and obey* is a nice broad concept that forms the basis for most—if not all—M/s relationships, but *service* and *obedience* are open to wide interpretation.

Also, people change over time. You may start an M/s relationships with one thing in mind but find that you're not with the right partner to pull it off. Either **you** have to change or that which you were trying to accomplish has to change. In the most general sense, all relationships begin with lust: after a while you'll have to decide whether the next stage is television or something else.

All that said, here are some examples of the characteristics of a few of the better-known M/s models that one finds today.

Structure One—Spiritual Model:
- Master is compassionate, but not overly concerned about slave's feelings
- Total obedience is assumed
- The couple lives and speaks in High Protocol
- slaves speak in third person
- slaves are only responsible to serve and to obey: sex may or may not be part of this equation
- slave is to empty itself of ego to enable Master to lead without resistance
- Uses M/s structure for spiritual purposes
- slave is property to be used as Master sees fit
- This is something like a monastic order in service to a higher power: frequently the service aspect of the relationship is focused on *giving back* to the Community (however that couple defines it)

Structure Two—Team Model:
- Leader/follower model; team model
- Based on compassion, reason, and empathetic guidance
- Few to no protocols: slave knows what slave needs to do
- Focus is on making the relationship more powerful than the separate people
- This is something like a business model of CEO/COO

Structure Three—Military Model:

- Military model: clearly hierarchical at all times.
- slave is expected to be a thinking individual who knows how to approach their superior with ideas and recommendations.
- Authority-based relationship that often uses protocols extensively: no interaction as equals.
- Master owns slave's time, attention, and future.
- Master often has legal safeguards in place for slave's future.
- Master is focused on ethical and compassionate leadership.
- slave's needs come before Master's wants, as Master needs to preserve slave's value within the operating unit.
- This is something like an 1880s upscale, formal marriage—but with consent

Structure Four—Public Media (or Fantasy) Model:

- Master makes all the rules and Master is never wrong (at least that's his public stance on the subject).
- Master's point of view is that slave is a living piece of property to be directed as Master sees fit.
- slave may not be permitted to bring much or any physical property into the relationship .
- Master has assumed only as much responsibility for this slave as Master wishes.
- slave's primary role is to serve Master's *wants*.
- slave has no personal autonomy and must always account for its actions.
- Master may tell slave how to dress, the kind of makeup/hair style to wear, and how to speak with Master or with others.
- slave is property to be used as Master sees fit.
- There are consequences (including dismissal) for failing to mould itself as Master directs.
- Master will not tolerate much freedom of thought or action.
- This is something like the vanillas' conceptualization of the porn model of M/s.

(Not that this is a test, but those of you who frequent the regional Master/slave conferences can probably put names with these management styles.)

Why do you think I just created that list?

Because, most relationships are a little of this and a little of that and at various points in this book you'll hear the voice of one or the other of these approaches speaking more loudly than another. In fact, you may be reading along in a section that largely speaks to one of these types of structures and stumble upon a comment that seems to be in almost direct opposition. The odd or discordant comment is intended to resonate with the reader who lives in one of the other types of structures. I've done that to continually remind you that *there is no one right way,* there is only the right way for you.

Characteristics of D/s and M/s relationship structures

Characteristics shared both by D/s and M/s relationships
- The roles of each partner have been pre-negotiated and there is an agreed-upon leader and follower.
- Most of the relationship parameters have been pre-negotiated and there are stated rules of behavior.
- There are consequences within the relationship for failure to comply with those rules.
- The s-type serves the wants and needs of the D-type.
- The s-type isn't supposed to go off *doing things* without first checking with the D-type.
- The D-type must exhibit above-average ethical and leadership behaviors so the s-type will continue to serve.

Characteristics more common in D/s structures
(Some of this material appears elsewhere in this book but is restated here because I'm grouping characteristics.)
- The submissive maintains personal authority over some areas of their life, such as work, biological family, religion, and possibly

the time they may spend on their own or doing something they (personally) want to do. They have discussed it and the Dom/me has agreed to it.

- The sub retains some amount of personal property as well as control of their own finances.
- Dominance is a key characteristic of the relationship: the relationship, itself, is about psychological dominance and submission.
- In the domain of love, *eros* (amorous love) and *philia* (friendship) are more of the focus than *agape* (making a conscious decision to love).

Characteristics more common in M/s structures

(Some of this material appears elsewhere in this book but is restated here because I'm grouping characteristics.)

- M/s structures often involve a written contract that defines the terms of the *offer* and *acceptance.*
- Master is 100% responsible for all aspects of the slave's well-being—mental health, physical health, finances, etc.
- The emphasis in the relationship is on *personal development.*
- Psychological dominance is not a requirement; ethical leadership is a requirement.
- In the domain of love, *agape* (making a conscious decision to love) and *philia* (friendship) are more of the focus than *eros* (amorous love).
- M/s relationships often involve a written code of personal and household protocols that describe the way the slave is to behave and the way the household is to run.
- The Master owns the slave's time and has been given authority by the slave to determine their future.
- The slave in an M/s relationship is really an extension of the Master's/Owner's will; an *advance-man* or *personal assistant.*
- The slave is expected to know the Master's wants, needs, and preferences as well as they know their own wants, needs, and preferences.
- The slave has transferred authority over itself to the Master: the slave can no longer refuse an ethical request by the Master without risking the Master terminating the entire relationship.

- The slave has no individual property or money: it all belongs to the Master.
- Most M/s structures stress the ethical code expressed as HILT: honor, integrity, loyalty, and trust. Words such as *focus, purpose,* and *intent* are common M/s topics.
- The overall relationship often includes a spiritual focus.
- M/s practitioners often refer to their relationship as a *Family* and often have extended Family members who are part of the House.

While one can make some general observations—as I've just done—the reality is that few authority-imbalanced relationships look alike. This is a prime example of an area where individual needs, preferences, and dreams create the details of an M/s couple's interaction. When it comes to demonstrating *structure* in relationships, you can have a dozen or so couples that all say that they live in a D/s, M/s, O/p, TPE kind of relationship yet appear to outsiders to behave somewhat to very differently. (O/p = Owner/property; TPE = Total Power Exchange)

Chapter 3
Who Are You?

Introspection. Let me start this section by putting this topic into some kind of personal context.

My first marriage lasted 17 years; my second marriage lasted 14 years: these were authority-equal relationships. They covered my life from age 28 to 56.

I went from totally vanilla to totally immersed in this lifestyle when I accidentally discovered the public scene in the summer of 2001. I joined two local BDSM clubs and started attending weekend BDSM and Leather conferences. After one year of experience, I petitioned my SM practice partner to be my Mistress. After we had been together about 18 months, she permitted me to have my own slave. None of us knew what we were doing: there was very little material available about BDSM and zero available about heterosexual Master/slave relationships. Guy Baldwin and Jack Rinella were the principal authors of M/s material at that time.

We lived as a threesome for seven of the next eight years, but by early in 2010, personal life issues for each of us had changed so much that the magic we had enjoyed for so many years went away.

It was then—early 2010—that I became reacquainted with Jen Fairfield; she is a strong dominant. Interestingly, she isn't a BDSM FemDomme;

her psychological orientation is much more like a female Leather Master. After two rugged years of emotional struggle between us (during which I wrote about 160,000 words of introspection and journaling and intensely studied the material that makes up the balance of this chapter), I felt a calling to serve her. I petitioned to be her slave in the summer of 2013. This caused something of a stir within my world, but I needed it: I needed to serve this woman: she is my muse. My personal challenge was to understand how I, as a dominant male, could serve someone more dominant than myself.

It was a difficult struggle.

To move myself from being vanilla to mastering physical SM skills to owning a slave for eight years to serving as a slave has taught me a thing or two. Psychological switching of this magnitude is enlightening. I feel I'm a better person for it.

As you can imagine, my *calling* led me to a great deal of introspection that then led to personal change. This chapter represents a summary of areas/topics that I found I needed to know in order to establish a stable M/s dynamic.

In most cases, I'm simply going to brush over an area to let you know that it's there. I leave it up to you to take each idea and adapt it (or not) to fit your own situation.

What do you need to feel satisfied?

Whether or not your realize it, you are totally in charge of yourself, your life, and your future. What you did five years ago, five months ago, five days ago, and yesterday have all led to who you are today. What you do today affects who you are tomorrow. In that light, *what do you need to do, who do you need to be* to feel satisfied and complete as a person?

If you were designing yourself, what would that design look like? In theory, at least, what might you change? How are you on social interactions? How are you on executive management skills? How are you on being a loving and supportive parent or spouse? How are your communication skills? In short, what do you think you need to be in order to quiet your inner voice of discontent?

I'm not suggesting that these answers come quickly or easily, I'm only suggesting that if you don't know your target, your goal, you haven't a chance in the world of hitting it. Also, I'm posing these questions to you as an individual, not as a couple. Once you've worked through such questions for yourself, the next challenge is to sit down with your Master or slave (and their similar list) and work out ways that you each can help the other... or do you even care?

This *do you care* question is central to this chapter. This chapter may not call to you if you view yourself as controlled by life's circumstances. The more curious you are about what makes you behave the way you behave, the more interesting you'll find this chapter.

Personal Control

Because people are not used to thinking about how they present themselves to the world, many find it challenging to decide where they fall on the dominant/submissive scale when it comes to entering into an authority-based relationship. I've not met many people who set out to change their English vocabulary, word choice, sentence structure, physical stance or vocal tonality as part of the process of becoming a more effective Master. I've not met many people who have analyzed their efficiency and effectiveness when completing Master's tasks. I've not met many couples who make a point of using active listening when speaking together in order to minimize misunderstandings. Fewer still have the (emotional) state management skills or acting training to control those aspects of themselves in order to present themselves purposefully one way or the other.

Are you interested in changing any of those aspects of your personality? Remember: you'll attract a partner who resonates with *who you are*. Interesting people attract interesting partners. When it comes to a relationship, you can be the kind of couple that nobody remembers, or you can be a power couple that lights up a room: it's up to you.

In a general sense, our personalities are affected by three major influences:
- Biological influences
  - Genetically determined temperament
  - Autonomic nervous system reactivity
  - Brain activity
- Psychological influences
  - Learned responses
  - Unconscious thought processes
  - Expectations and interpretations (tied to *projection* that we'll eventually cover)
- Socio-cultural influences
  - Childhood experiences
  - Situational influences
  - Cultural expectations
  - Social support

Once you start to dice it up this way, though, you'll be surprised how much control you actually have over yourself and your personality.

You probably can't do much with biological influences (such as your underlying tendency towards depression) without meds, but within the M/s dynamic you can affect most of the others.
- Psychological influences
  - Learned responses can be changed and unlearned
  - Unconscious thought processes can be controlled through meditation and mindfulness
  - Expectations and interpretations give way to strategies such as *not having any expectations* of outcomes and *reframing* your reactions to events (you can look up "reframing" on the Internet).
- Socio-cultural influences
  - Childhood experiences—therapy?
  - Situational influences—taking the time to be sure that what you *think* happened (or is going on) is verifiably accurate before formulating your response. Change your perspective from being at the effect of events to being in control of your response to events.

- o Cultural expectations—whose culture? Vanilla or MAsT?
- o Social support—you're in control of this one: build your helping network differently or better if you don't like it now.

Which means that, "If it's going to be, it's up to me!" You are god in your own universe.

What role do you want to play in life?

Do you want to be a leader or follower? Do you want to be the person doing the explaining or the person listening to others explain? What archetype calls to you? If you look up Carolyn Myss's work, you'll find a starting point for understanding yourself and your actions in relation to common archetypes. From her Website, here is an abbreviated list to consider:

Actor	Dreamer	Networker	Seductress
Anarchist	Fool	Patriarch	Servant
Bureaucrat	Healer	Poet	Sidekick
Caregiver	Historian	Priest	Storyteller
Companion	Knight	Prophet	Thief
Crone	Magician	Rebel	Tyrant
Detective	Matriarch	Sadist	Visionary
Diplomat	Muse	Scholar	Wizard

We all have fantasies. For some, our fantasies mostly concern our world of work: the jobs we'd like, the kinds of people with whom we'd like to work, and how long or short the trip to our ideal workplace would be. For others, our fantasies look further outward to dreams about how we'd like to help others, help our communities, and help the world in general. We have relationship fantasies, travel fantasies, financial fantasies, sadistic fantasies. However, for this section of this book, I want to focus on *relationship fantasies*.

When you think of fantasies about your personal social-sexual fantasies, what comes to mind? Boyfriend/girlfriend? Master/Mistress? Dom/Domme? Daddy, Top, Trainer? submissive, boy/boi/girl? Pet? slave?

Related to this—are you interested in the role you would play, the person you would be if you were playing that role full time, or both? Here's the distinction: I may enjoy playing some role within my relationship that is actually not a role that I assume in real life—it's clearly a fun fantasy role. On the other hand, I may find that I *like* the role that I play within my relationship and decide to develop it further in order to carry that role out past my relationship and into my workplace. Big difference.

So let's keep this discussion contained for a bit. Let's presume that you're really fantasizing about your role only within your relationship. That brings up three questions:
- What is your role now?
- What would you like your role to be?
- How do you get from here to there?

That brings up a couple of harder questions:
- Do you have a history of succeeding at getting what you set your heart on?
- If you don't have a history of success, why not? What are you creating in your world that is holding you back? Again, there are many, many courses and paths to help you with this line of questioning; I can only raise this as a point to consider.

Here's where I'm going with this…

If your fantasy role within your relationship doesn't work out, are you willing to consider reinventing a role for yourself and give it another shot? If *Master* doesn't work, how about *Lord*, or *Sir*, or *Daddy*, or *Uncle*? Are you willing to try new paths? Are you willing to change for the sake of the person with whom you're in a relationship? Are you willing to remove the emotional loading on "failing" at that relationship role in order to cleanly (without emotional baggage) move on to try out another relationship role?

These are all questions of personal security, risk, and adventuresomeness (yes, I know that's not a word, but it fits; I'm demonstrating "being adventuresome" in text).

Roles and functionality

What you call yourself affects what you expect of yourself every bit as much as what others expect from you. If you call yourself a pet, nobody is expecting slave behaviors out of you. If you're being a slave, nobody is expecting you to curl up at your Master's feet and start rubbing your head against their leg.

The following s-type roles carry expectations about different kinds of service that would be expected:
- Slave
- Servant
- Major domo
- Butler
- Valet
- Household manager
- Personal assistant

The following D-type roles carry expectations about different kinds of management that would be expected:
- Owner
- Master/Mistress
- Daddy/Mommy
- Manager
- Guide
- Boss
- King/Queen
- Lord/Lady
- Dom/me

You may think of yourself as X but really be carrying out the functions of Y. Similarly, you may think that by describing your relationship role as X, you don't have responsibilities for Z.

Just material for you to consider...

Multiple roles

Whether your Household is two people or twenty-two people, many find that they have different roles in different settings. Life is dynamic; relationships are dynamic. The way your Family interacts on a lovely day when the sun is shining is vastly different than how it interacts as you're fleeing for your lives in the face of a tornado.

In large Households, you may find that Master can have a slave with whom he has sex, a slave only for service, and a puppy for a pet. Then, again, you may keep a boy/boi around who only needs some nurturing growth. As you earn respect within your community you may find yourself petitioned to Master one or more people who are seen less frequently than the household slaves. There are so many roles that one can play within the overall M/s dynamic that I can't really do that topic justice. This is a world where you can stretch yourself. You can be different people to different people. You can express yourself differently as a function of your different relationships.

It's also a world in which formal protocols help to reinforce the negotiated roles each of you has chosen. (Yes, Master abides by protocols as much as slave, even though Master may think that Master is just acting *naturally*. What Master thinks of as *natural behavior* is the visible representation of Master's *Book of Life* that has been created from a lifetime of experiences. Master is likely to find that actually writing them down may break open some new ways of thinking about him/herself so the s-type doesn't have to develop so many work-arounds.)

Critical Observation:

As a general rule, "A" leaders select "A" players because they are confident in their own abilities and are used to being surrounded by excellence.

However—again as a general rule—"B" leaders select "C" players because they can't risk being exposed as "B" leaders rather than as "A" leaders.

On ego and insecurity in relationships

Okay, I'm going to go out on a limb, here. I'm going to apply some really sensitive business wisdom to choosing a mate in an M/s setting. I'm not sure whether I hope nobody reads this, or whether I hope a lot of people read this. But, I will say this: when I look for a partner, I specifically look for an "A" type.

In a business environment, this plays out as follows: It's better to have an "A" team with a "B" plan, than a "B" team with an "A" plan. This business idea probably was derived from an old Arab proverb: *An army of sheep lead by a lion would defeat an army of lions led by a sheep*. In a personal environment, my experience has been that an insecure D-type will take a **weaker, less secure s-type** as a partner in order to be able to control the person without being called on his/her act. Yes, two "A" players can find themselves butting heads from time to time, but that's where the leader's authority confronts the slave's commitment to follow.

I've actually seen this situation unfold in real life. A close friend of mine was faced with having to choose to marry one of two women. Although successful in business and investments, he selected the weaker, less self-actualized woman because he, himself, was insecure about relations with women. His choice astonished his close friends at the time. The woman could never quite get on the same page with him; he finally gave up trying and resigned himself to the situation. (My cynical aphorism about such situations is that: *You can't make a silk purse out of a sow's ear unless you start with a silk sow*.)

Are you both really okay?
Perception drives relationships.

That means not only do you react to your interpretation of the ways others behave around you, but they react to their interpretation of the way you act. People have varying degrees of control over themselves and the ways that they act. Some people are more okay than others.

But, what is "okay," anyway? Each of us knows people who seem a little *off*. They do things that just don't seem to be right for the situation. They don't appear—to **you**—as having quite the right responses to situations. They seem to piss a lot of people off. Worse, they don't seem to get it. You may be partnered with a person like this.

So far as anyone can tell, these people think that *they* are okay and that it's *others* who are not quite right in the head. Sound familiar? Of course, most of us think we see the world correctly and that others don't, but I'm now speaking about people who could legitimately be referred to a psychologist.

They may not be neuro-typical: purportedly about one in 300 adult men fall somewhere on the Autism Spectrum Disorder scale (for example, I have Asperger Syndrome). Or, a person's emotional baggage may be affecting personal and work relationships. Or, they may have some underlying behavior difficulty…

- They may have an oppositional behavior pattern—you say A, they say not-A.
- They may be passive-aggressive: they say "yes" but have no intention of doing what was asked.
- They may be *takers* rather than *givers*; users.
- They may *sort-by-self* rather than *sort-by-others*; is hedonistic. (Note: "sort-by-self" means that when you're presented with a surprise situation you immediately think about how **you** will be affected by that situation rather than how others would be affected. Successful customer-relations personnel fall into the other camp: they "sort-by-others" and can easily express empathy. This concept is a close relative to "inward looking vs. outward looking" in terms of a relationship.)

Because many people don't really understand how they, themselves, work, they can't quite figure out how YOU work. More troubling, it may be hard to realize that someone close to you has these kinds of issues going on because you may be too close to them to be objective. You keep excusing the behavior or simply hoping it won't reoccur.

How can you become who you want to be?

So: once you have identified who you are, the next stage is to identify with precision who you'd like to be. Identifying who you'd like to be will enable you to put a program together that will slowly change the way you interact in the world. Whether you are an s-type or a D-type, this process can be helped or hindered quite a bit depending upon whether or not your M/s relationship is structured for personal growth and development.

What interpersonal, technical and life skills do you bring to the table?

Before I begin this section, a comment: I've heard people say that they've had (let us say) five years of experience at some skill, yet when you observe them at that skill, they don't appear to be very good at it. I've heard other people say they've been living in a Master/slave structure for (let us say) five years but they've never read any books about it. From this, I've learned to distinguish between someone who has had one year of experience that they repeated five times versus someone who has had five years of progressive experience leading to skill or knowledge mastery. I further draw the conclusion that some people are dead-set to learn little or nothing from life's experiences and will go out of their way to do so.

So, here are some tough questions—tough, in large part because few people spend the time to think them through before starting a new relationship or maintaining the one they're in. Starting right now and lasting throughout this book, I'm going to be putting forth questions designed to cause you to stop and think. And—with any luck—act. I'll provide tips and techniques and nudges as they fit in, but you MAY have to seek out experts and courses to build your strength in certain fields.

What are the components of your personality?

In M/s, the better a Master understands his/her own life/reality filters the easier it is to understand who your slave is. You have to know who your slave is in order to know the strategies and approaches you'll need to train that person.

Unless you and your partner have fairly similar education and work backgrounds, chances are that the two of you solve problems somewhat-to-very differently. To the extent that you think/problem-solve differently, you will experience some relationship stress points. I've been through this a couple of times and my suggestion to you is to consider putting yourself and your partner (or intended partner) through a battery of self-tests. I pass this tip on to you because I, at least, found it very helpful to have some objective measures to help me figure out how I work and how my partner works. In my opinion, it's worth spending the money to take these—and other—personality tests.

What are the Meyers-Briggs scores for you and your partner? Have you studied how *your* type gets along with *their* type? (Once you have your scores, the book *Please Understand Me* explains how someone with one score is most likely to interact with someone with another score. This is really useful information.)

How do you take in (process) information? There are a number of ways that you can think about the way you learn. One of the most common ways of cutting this topic describes three basic modalities in which we convert information to memory: visual (learning by seeing), auditory (learning by hearing), and kinesthetic (learning by doing). Most people use one predominant modality, but some use a balance between two or even all three. As it relates to structured relations, not only must you be in touch with the way YOU learn, but also be sensitive to the ways your current or potential partner learns.

What are your preferred *working styles*? Are you mostly a *fact finder* or are you mostly good at *follow through*? Are you a *quick start* or are you better as an *implementer*? I have found that the Kolbe A test *(www.kolbe.com)* is extremely helpful for revealing how people work. I was able to use the Kolbe A results to help me work much more smoothly with my partner—whose scores were vastly different from mine.

Here's a true story: The person who introduced me to Neuro-Linguistic Programming (NLP—the communication method that teaches how to communicate directly to a person's preferred *learning modality*) commented that until he understood about this process, he would get furious at his wife for coming up behind him and putting her hands on his shoulders while he was reading at his desk. His NLP studies revealed to him that his wife communicated love through touch (kinesthetic communication style) and that her touch was intended as a love message. He, though, was a highly visual learner who would become completely absorbed in reading. The act of being touched at that time not only broke his concentration, but also broke his emotional state—he tested as *low-kinesthetic* and didn't like to be touched.

There are many ways of learning how you and/or your partner understand things. For more information about learning styles, try an Internet search on "learning modalities."

What are you good at? What aren't you good at?

As the Master, do you want a slave whose skills complement you or supplement you? Do you want someone who is pretty good in the same areas where you are pretty good (sports, home repair, business dealings, etc) or do you want a partner who has skill proficiency in areas that you don't. As a slave, do you prefer leading in areas where you have personal competency or would you rather not lead but follow and support your Master in areas that the Master leads you?

There are a number of free online assessment tools, just search for "skills-inventory tests." One that I personally like is *www.rileyguide. com/assess.html.*" They have a number of interesting tests that are designed to help you figure out your areas of strength and weakness. As with personality tests, I recommend that you look these over to see whether any can be useful in better understanding yourself and your partner.

Been married?

In many ways, our BDSM culture is kinder to you if you've already been married. Generally, those who have been married have discovered how to live in close quarters with someone under a variety of good and bad situations. If you're still married and both of you wish to explore this path, so much the better, for you both have your eyes open and you're starting this adventure together. Good for you.

Now, if you are married and have discovered that you have a calling not shared by your partner, you now have some also good information, but you also may now have a bit of a problem, for whether or not one is *kinky* is a fact of life and fighting against it, denying it, will have ramifications in other parts of your life.

So—what if you've been married?

How did that work out? Are you still friends with your husband/wife? Is there more than one ex? Were there similar problems with each marriage? Are you carrying problems from one mate to the next? How could you change to make this new relationship different from prior relationships? Without changing yourself, have you ever considered that *this is as good as it gets*?

What's causing the breakups? Have you spent time thinking about what went wrong? Have you had help thinking this through—been through some therapy? If yes, can you express what you learned and how you changed? If not, what makes you think you won't repeat the patterns you went through before?

Did you nurture your prior spouse or partner? Can you explain how they developed under your care—either as the Dominant or submissive in the relationship? Did YOU do all the growing? Did THEY do all the growing? (*Growing* relates to continuing to expand your spiritual, intellectual, and social skills.)

What will you do *this time* that will be different? What have you learned over the years that will give you a good shot at doing things differently this time? Remember Albert Einstein's observation that the definition of insanity is: "Doing the same thing over and over again and expecting different results."

Remember: there are ample examples of people who go from one marriage into the next and the second marriage fails much as the first. Reason: unless you are a person who specifically is working on changing core aspects of *who you are,* you are most likely to bring the behavioral baggage you've gathered throughout your life from one marriage into the next, with similar results. That's why *real change* is internal and not external—and it's why it is so hard to do. You are largely blind to the subtle oddities that make up your personality. You've learned to be happy with yourself and have trouble understanding why you should give up some of those beloved idiosyncrasies for this other person.

What does your work history look like?
Your work history tells you quite a bit about your relationship history. If you are well liked at work, chances are that you're well liked at home. If you have trouble keeping a job, chances are that you have trouble keeping a partner. On the positive side, you have the opportunity to use your work hours as practice sessions for your home life: improve one and you'll improve the other.

At work, you have continual opportunities to improve your social skills. In the larger sense, you can learn to be a leader; you can learn to be impeccable in your word; you can learn to speak using *active listening* skills (summarizing what someone says to you to be sure that you understood them correctly before replying). In the smaller sense, you can learn how to augment your understanding of others by understanding body language; you can learn how to lead by asking questions; you can learn to remove emotional words from your replies to others.

Work settings provide outstanding opportunities to stretch your abilities to get along with people. Do you have to work with a difficult person? Consider taking that on as a challenge and research ways that you can change yourself so the other person grows to find you easy to work with. Work with someone who just doesn't understand you? Consider studying listening and speaking styles. Do you have to work on a team that just can't seem to work together? Consider studying team-building skills and techniques.

You'll need every one of these skills as you work with your partner, whether your partner is your Master or your slave.

In the business world, people are not really paid to work; they are paid to solve problems. To the extent that you can solve problems, you are valuable within your workforce. The process of solving problems is often complex: problems are solved when both parties feel that they have won something. To figure out a solution that enables others to win involves developing visionary skills. Visionary skills—a complex topic in its own right—combines such skills as empathy, encyclopedic knowledge of your own as well as the other person (or company's) operating environment, and close monitoring and analysis of the results of everything that you try out in your effort to craft the win-win solution.

You will maintain your M/s relationship for the same basic reason a business remains in business: it is perceived as bringing value to others. As the value equation shifts within your M/s relationship, the two (or more) of you will feel more or less stable.

Unless you are a visionary leader at work, how do you become a visionary leader in your relationship? Ah! Homework!!

On choosing a mate

I'm going to begin this part of the book by taking a broader view of an authority-imbalanced relationship and concentrate on some lessons from the *vanilla* world—slightly augmented by my own comments. On several occasions, I've watched negotiations for an M/s relationship break down when the Master would present the potential slave with a long list of *demands and conditions* prior to spending any time with the person first, in order to determine whether or not they even wanted a relationship with them to begin with. Said differently, the Master wanted the slave candidate to skip the *getting to know you* stage of relationship-building process in favor of the *here's how you must obey me or else* stage. Needless to say, these self-called Masters spent a lot of time churning through slave candidates.

So, here, for your consideration, are some general relationship guidelines that apply to people on both sides of the slash. These notes are really superficial, though, and if any of these ideas seem to hit a chord in you, I'd encourage you to do more research/searching.

Attributes for the long term

Think of yourself as an older Master. Think of yourself as 75. Okay, try 83. You're probably not having much sex. Your slave's skin is getting thin and fragile, so you have had to stop the flogging; whips went away years ago. What's remaining? What core values are there for you to rely upon? What bonds the two of you? You have to make this list. I can only tell you that you are VERY likely to find yourself in this situation. You can take that one to the bank. Doing a little work now will save you a lot of regrets later.

Flip the situation. You're still the 75 year-old Master, but now you're being viewed through your slave's eyes: what core values and steady behaviors bind the two of you? When your slave reflects on the last five years, does he/she express a dreamy and satisfied look of fulfillment, or a hardened look of a life not lived very satisfyingly.

So, here is a little list of personal attributes for you to consider:
- Kindness
- Loyalty
- Insight
- Flexibility/adaptability
- Devotion
- Financial competence—the ability of the mate to hold down a responsible job

Curiosity: When you expect to be with someone a long time, you may want someone who goes out into the world and brings back ideas for new experiences. You may get tired of doing all the leading or all the serving. What characteristics would you want in a partner that supports your core need in this arena?
- Can the person expand to develop their potentials? Do they even know their own powers?
- Are they quick to want to learn new things? Do they reach *toward* a goal or *away from* a potential challenge to their *status quo*?
- Can they see old things in new ways?
- Are they curious about life?

Passion: Be passionate about something. And, I suggest that you choose someone who has similar passions—similar interests in making memories. You may need to draw on the good memories during hard times. I also suggest that you choose someone who makes your life bigger, not smaller. Consider selecting a person who is curious about the world around them.

Values: Choose someone with similar values. There are many relationship models, some of which are quite unusual. You should understand something about these different models as early in the relationship as possible, and make sure your intended partner has both a similar understanding and a similar model in mind. At an extremely broad cut, some relationship models are:
- Open vs. closed sexual relationship (one or both partners can have other casual sexual partners)
- Monogamy vs. polyamory (multiple long term partners)
- Power exchange vs. equal partners

Selective blindness: Learn to overlook certain traits. Sometimes, little things that initially were attractive/cute will become annoying over time. I'm not suggesting that you overlook character flaws such as criminal activity or dishonesty; you can't build a relationship with someone once serious character flaws are revealed. But, I am suggesting that in the larger scope of your lives together, there may be certain annoyances that may be better left alone. After all, your partner is likely to be putting up with a bunch of crap from you, too.

Amicability: Be able to laugh at yourself; have lots of friends. This usually indicates friendliness, flexibility and openness. Good attributes in a mate. You will appreciate these traits in a slave and your slave will appreciate these traits in you.

Compassion: When you pass someone who is clearly less fortunate than yourself (perhaps a street person), what is your reaction? What is your potential partner's reaction? Are either of you repulsed or do you feel empathy? In an important way, this reaction can give you a window into how the other person thinks about others: do they generally seek to include others and see good in everyone or do they tend to seclude those who do not fit their screening criteria—overweight, physically unattractive, poorly dressed, speak poorly, etc.

You may find that a person who has trouble expressing compassion for others less fortunate may have trouble connecting emotionally with YOU or certain aspects of you. Or, this may be an indicator that you may have trouble plugging in to your own partner or potential partner. Is your potential mate willing to listen to you? Truly listen? Do YOU listen? How do you know you're really listening?

Mutual attraction: *Conventional Wisdom*, should such a thing exist, says that in the best of all worlds, a relationship works because you match cerebrally, physically, and sexually. That means that you like the way the other person thinks and you respect both the depth and breadth of their knowledge AND that you like the way they express themselves.

In the kinky world we add another element: that your kinks match.

What brings the two of you together? Do you both like horse races? Mountaineering? Books? Partying? Kinky play?

- Are YOU sensitive? Is this potential partner sensitive? Are they alert to things around the two of you when you are together? Are you as interested in **how** your partner thinks as much as you're interested in **what** he/she thinks?

  [This is a fine point, and I'll expand it a bit. In this country, one of the key differences between the handful of elite private colleges and the vast number of other post-secondary institutions is that the elite institutions teach you *how to think*, while the others only offer courses about *what to think*. That's why certain branches of the government and certain kinds of corporations are so eager to employ graduates of those schools. Presuming you did *not* attend one of those kinds of special educational institutions (and I did not) there is still quite a bit that you can now do. There are lots of resources—books, courses, and Internet material—that help teach you how to think through issues and problems. I recommend those to you. It's an interesting Path in its own right.]

- How do each of you react to the other person's personal space—home or apartment? Do each of you compliment the other on decorations, or are you (or your partner-candidate) fairly oblivious to them? Because personal décor is an outward expression of the inner person, this is an important point. Among other things, the presence or absence of items on walls and throughout one's living space helps others to understand how you take in information—see item #9, below—and can be an important insight into another person.

Independence: Choose someone who has an inner life, someone on their own journey, someone independent of you. This person should see you as a partner on their journey, too.

Personally, I distinguish between *wanting* and *needing* someone. If you *need them*, you are at the *effect* of the relationship—that is, you don't come from *choice* and you are unusually vulnerable. If you feel you *need* your mate, chances are you're going to run into some problems within a structured relationship: the Master may have trouble giving unpleasant orders out of fear of alienating the slave; the slave may have to compromise some core needs in order to appear to be compliant within the structure lest the Master end the relationship.

Processing emotional hurt

When you hurt someone, they feel pain and often show it clearly enough for you to recognize what happened. When they hurt you, you feel pain and often show it clearly enough for them to recognize what happened. The question is: how does each of you care for (emotionally heal) the other when you've hurt one another? Effectively handling emotional pain you cause another is an important aspect of maturity and vital in a stable relationship.

So… what do *you* do?

- Do you clam up—indicating that you don't know how to process the pain you have given your partner?
- Do you go into some form of stylized speech pattern, indicating your own emotional instability or social immaturity?
- Do you become angry/defensive when you realize that you've hurt someone?

As an example, my own challenges reading emotional feelings in others led me to use and recommend the Native American practice of "talking sticks" to work through upsets. Either person may request a session. The hurt party picks up the stick and talks until he/she is done. The stick then passes to the other party, who speaks until done. The person holding the stick may not be interrupted. To be sure that the communication is clear, the person listening to their partner must repeat what they hear their partner saying before offering a counterpoint. This goes on until the issue is resolved. Another person who uses this system explained that over the years it got so that the talking sticks only had to be used when both people were emotionally involved with an issue. Otherwise, the person who was not the aggrieved party could easily sit quietly while the upset partner expressed their hurt.

Processing/sorting information

Note: This section is adapted from my earlier books: *Master/slave Relations: Communication 401—the Advanced Course* and *Master/slave Relations: Solutions 402—Living in Harmony).* I recommend those books to you because they provide a more thorough discussion of topics that are coming up in this section of this book. However, since this material is so important to this book as well, I've cut out everything that I could and included the core ideas, here.

Mismatches in the ways a couple process information can doom a relationship, whether it's a business relationship or a personal relationship. The relationship is at risk when one person has trouble getting (hearing with understanding) the other person's messages. One or both of you will become hurt/frustrated/angry when basic communication breaks down for no apparent reason. Worse, this difficulty usually becomes more acute during emotional upsets—just the time you need communication clarity.

But, there is relationship risk even without upsets. If one person is high-visual and the other is high-kinesthetic but neither of you know about differences in information processing modalities, then the ways each of you communicate love or respect for the other may not coincide. That can be a problem. It can even be a problem that ultimately splits the two of you apart, as neither of you quite feels loved.

Because I expand these points later when I speak about slave training, I'll only take a paragraph here for an overview.

People process information according to some combination of the five senses: sight, hearing, touch, taste, smell. Some people understand better when *listening* to new information, other people need to *see the plan laid out.* Still others are kinesthetic learners and tend to take lots of notes in order to anchor what they are hearing. Those who remember things by taste are likely to want to express their love by preparing elegant meals, while those who tie smells to their memories will be sensitive both to the smells in your home and also to the scent/perfume you use. (Someone who associates smells with emotions probably sniffed your neck early in your relationship. You evidently passed that test.)

Love languages

If you have not recently read Gary Chapman's book *The Five Love Languages: How to Express Heartfelt Commitment to Your Mate* I urge you to do so. He makes a compelling argument that people are brought up learning how to express love to others in a particular way—a way that may not match the way your partner was brought up to express love. Your question: "Are you saying *I love you* in a way that your partner can get it?" Here is a list of Chapman's main categories.

- **Money/gifts:** Some men feel that turning their paychecks over to their spouse, or buying gifts, is a demonstration of *I love you* and that they don't have to *say* anything.
- **Sensory:** Some people respond to verbal cues, some to touch, some to visual cues. Work this out before you begin a committed relationship, or at least be able to translate the differences for them.
- **Performing services:** Some people translate the neatness/tidiness of the house as *I love you*. Others translate the way you can plan a trip as *I love you*.
- **Time and attention:** Some people consider that spending a lot of time with them translates to *I love you*. For such people, reducing the amount of time you spend with them— or threatening to leave them—may trigger substantial abandonment issues that they have experienced since childhood.
- **Verbal:** Some people respond most strongly to being *told* that they are loved. In fact, they may also need to bet told out loud that they are doing a good job as your partner/friend/lover. Failing to acknowledge them may cause them to worry that they are not pleasing you.

What will you do to make your relationship magical?

Okay, since we've now explored questions about what you're looking for—in the lifestyle and in the person—now it's time to ask how much are you willing to pay to get what you want? How much are you willing to pay to transform yourself into what you suspect that you can be? How much are you willing to pay over that amount to support your *partner* as they transform into what you want them to be? If you're the slave and you don't feel that you have the right or the control to change your Master, that brings up another on/off type decision: are you willing to partner with someone who remains just as they are now for the balance of your time together? In the alternative, how much of your own energy are you willing to pour into buffing and polishing the diamond in the rough with whom you have aligned yourself?

And… if you're the Master reading this, don't for one minute think I'm speaking solely of what it's going to cost you to get your *partner* to operate in the fashion YOU wish—that's only half of it. It is very likely going to take time and money in order to add to your own personal skills and those of your mate.

Think I'm sounding like a preachy parent? Well, chances are that by the time you're reading this I'm somewhat past 70 years old. I've been around the block a time or two. Age carries with it the weight of experience.

When I worked for the Justice Department's research division I once overheard someone say:

> What we have is not what we want;
> What we want is not what we need;
> What we need costs too much.

I wrote it down at the time, realizing that there was a truth in there that I needed to think about. I've thought of it often, since, and concluded that this is a *core reality* in life. It applies, here, because it takes a certain amount of hard (purposeful) work and frustration to move yourselves from being two individuals to being a *team*.

When you're thinking about the amount of work involved in changing someone to operate within a culture different to the one they grew up in, think about the U.S. Military. They put recruits through Boot Camp; now think of the Drill Sergeants, not the recruits. Do you, as the Master, have the personality, background, and training to train another? If not, you may have to learn some serious personnel management techniques. Oh. *Marine Boot Camp* is too extreme? Okay, how about *team leader* within the sales or marketing division of an established company. You have a team of seven people who have never worked together: what, exactly, are you going to do? Possible answers: read books, take courses, and find a mentor…

From the slave's side, not only do they have to master routine protocols (see, for example, *Protocol Handbook for the Leather slave: Theory and Practice* by Robert J. Rubel, PhD), but they also have to master immediate and graceful obedience to Master's commands. As we're not brought up in a culture where grace and elegance in service are expected (as they would be had we been brought up in an Oriental culture), this may take some patience over time. Of course, these are just examples: as the Master, you may not want to be served with grace and elegance. That's the beauty of these kinds of unusual/ unique relationships; you get to make up the internal rules.

Do you currently describe your life and your relationship(s) as *magical*? If not, why not? It's your life, and it's your responsibility to make it magical. It's okay if it's not magical right now—you're in charge of it and can change many aspects of it immediately. It doesn't take a lot of money; it takes *having the idea that you can change*. It can start as simply as doing Internet searches in areas such as "how to change myself and expand from there."

Unless you can imagine it, you can't create it. And, failing to take charge of your life and your relationship(s) can cause you to feel that you are *at the effect* of being stuck in a particular life circumstance in your work, your interests, or with your particular partner(s). What I mean by *at the effect* is that you are not *at the cause*—you are not the creative force behind your own life; you have adjusted to the conditions, rather than adjusting the conditions to meet your own needs.

This last point brings us back to the *imagination* issue raised a few pages earlier. You have to be able to conceive of something— you have to be able to write it out as a goal—in order to make it real. Many things first have to be thought out before they can be converted to reality. If you

> The danger lies in imprisoning ourselves within our definitions of experience.
>
> —David Boorstein, Librarian of Congress

don't hold the *concept* of something, it's hard to dream it up. There are many common examples of this when it comes to language—just think back to training a young child not to touch a hot stove: the child must first understand such concepts as *hot, hurt,* and *stove* etc.

You don't know what you don't know: blind spots creep into your life and your relationships. If you can't imagine a different set of conditions, then you can't work toward them. In my personal life, I have many times joined some group simply because it was against my nature to join such a group. I was in an international service club for many years for that reason. I joined a square dance club—and lasted five years—for that reason. I will sometimes explore a new relationship with someone who does NOT fit my personal sense of a good fit for that reason.

So, my message is: work to stretch your experiences so that you can grow your imagination. The richer your imagination, the richer your life.

And, this brings me back to another key question to consider: What's your level of commitment to an authority-imbalanced relationship— are you interested in living this way 24/7 or are you exploring M/s structures as a form of scene-specific BDSM play? One is not better than the other, but one involves more expense of time and money than the other. Let me address this topic to two distinct audiences: those readers who are currently in an M/s relationship, and those who are reading this book and considering whether or not to enter into an M/s relationship.

If you are **currently** in an M/s relationship, the *investment* question probably centers on your mutual growth or on skills that you or your slave could attain that would benefit (put sparkle into) your relationship. This endless list could include topics such as:

For the Master
- Read books about (and attend mini-courses on) self-improvement or business skills (public speaking, running a meeting, time management, personnel management).
- Travel and learn about the world
- Learn to dance
- Start going to theater and concerts
- Get certified in advanced first aid and CPR
- Take improv acting classes

For the slave
- Gain social skills about maintaining interesting conversation
- Learn to play an instrument
- Learn how to entertain more formally
- Learn massage therapy
- Improve cooking skills
- Become a master at giving sexual pleasure—strengthen your pelvic floor muscles (either gender, actually), fellatio skills, etc.
- Prepare a *slave's Book* that records all Master's particular preferences—create checklists for all repeatable processes (packing before a trip, preparing for a dinner party, etc.).

If you are **exploring** the idea of starting an M/s relationship I'll assume that you've obtained this book because you think that a *structured relationship* makes sense for you. If you're at the front-end of a relationship, you have time to consider some big picture issues. My strong recommendation is to write out—as clearly as possible—what you absolutely **must** have in a slave (or a Master). Start by writing out your expectations of each person's role and responsibilities. Next, write out those skills you want this person to possess—then look for a person with most or all of those skills already in hand. This is a far more rapid and less costly process than taking a person and trying to retrain them in your image. People tend not to change much over time, so if you can find someone who already mostly behaves in ways that please you and already possesses most of the skills you're looking for, you're way ahead of the game.

Importantly, because of the *authority transfer* aspect of an M/s relationship, the slave is not in a very good position to retrain Master—easier to find one already made to fit your own preferences.

What if it doesn't work out?

Sometimes a relationship just doesn't work and you have to break it off to avoid damaging both people. This is as true in vanilla relationships as in kinky ones. However, it can be a little worse in this culture because—for many of us—we've invested a great deal of emotional energy, time, and study to *getting it right* either as Master or slave.

One time, I was counseling a women who had become a close kink friend. She had just gone through a break-up and said to me: "When you first realize that the relationship isn't going to work out, you feel that you've flunked the slave test." (Stormy Nights, private conversation) I get it.

I've put this section in this part of the book because it is part of *knowing one's self*.

You have to know when to hold 'em,
know when to fold 'em,
know when to walk away,
know when to run…

—From the song The Gambler written by Don Schlitz and sung by Kenny Rogers

Because people become involved in relationships (of any kind) for their own reasons, it's not possible to project why one specific relationship fails after some time. To quote Master Skip Chasey: "A Master is willing to bear, without complaint or self-pity, the awareness that doing his best may at times not be good enough." (Master Skip Chasey: *The Qualities of a Realized Master*, handout material)

Let me hasten to add: You have many options to consider when a structured relationship doesn't work out.
- Change yourself and your expectations of your respective roles;
- Change the *type* of structure (from Master/slave to Dom/sub or Trainer/pet or...)
- Accept that this form of relationship does not meet your own needs and return to vanilla
- Etc.

I argue for trying to find another way because—after all—you must have felt something *substantial* to have offered (or accepted) the training contract in the first place. Build on the common elements, rather than dismiss the entire relationship. Don't throw the baby out with the bathwater.

Personally, I have had the experience of extending a three-month training contract to a potential slave, only to discover, at about the 60-day point, that the person did not have a slave heart. She wanted the relationship to work so badly that she worked very hard to conform to my version of an M/s relationship; we realized that we were on the wrong path. However, rather than end our relationship, we restructured it as a form of Daddy/girl relationship (ours was an Uncle/niece structure). This worked just fine and lasted another nine months. This structure had the added advantage of being much less threatening to my Alpha slave.

But, if the relationship does have to end, if you can't agree on a different structure, all that your friends need to know is that *the contract ended*. Nothing else. "Didn't you want to renew it?" asked a well-meaning friend. "No, we were complete with our relationship and the contract period ended." End of story.

Chapter 4
What do you Want?

Okay, you've decided to prepare for an unusual relationship structure, even if you aren't yet sure of your options. You may not know whether you want to scene the roles or live the roles. Not a problem: before we get into selecting a partner there are a few initial steps to go through.

You might want to explore a threshold question: does your slave candidate want to be a 24/7 slave or something else? For the sake of this section, I'll assume you want what is increasingly called, *Total Power Exchange*—a 24/7 relationship that involves power exchange, as opposed to scene-specific role-play. From this point, the greatest hurdle is the candidate's personal honesty. You are going to have to discern what sings to this person—what he/she really wants out of this relationship with you. Is this slave really prepared for an *authority transfer* in which you, as Master, now have nearly absolute control? You may want your slave candidate to think this through for a minute. The slave may love jazz, and Master only listens to rap. How will that work? In fact, how will your candidate react when you elect not to allow your slave to listen to the radio or to CDs at all? Be assured, I decide on my slave's wardrobe, hair color and style, nail color, car choice, and use of time.

And, this is NOT *micromanagement*. It's a case of the Master wishing their life to be a certain way and using the slave to support those intentions. Is your candidate clear that once he/she enters into a

Master/slave relationship 24/7, all rights to make personal choices are forfeit? For example, if your slave tells you that he/she is going out on errands to point A, B and C, I expect that YOU expect that the slave will only to go to points A, B and C. How are you going to react if your slave decides to stop in at point D? Do you take that as a good sign of initiative, or do you take it as an incredible exercise of free will? Do you expect a phone call from the slave asking whether or not you will allow him/her to add in the extra stop, or are you satisfied so long as the slave explains why the extra stop was necessary? (My answer, by the way, was that the extra stop was an incredible and inexcusable exercise in the very kind of free will that the slave no longer possesses. The slave made that stop by taking time away from me.)

Of course, this is what we're discussing throughout this book.

The slave's role is to be of service to Master. Master's role is to cherish the slave and ensure the slave's well being in all regards. Ideally, it's a synergistic relationship: one plus one equals five, not just three. The combination of the two of you produces a magical result that is better than either of you could obtain on your own.

Pretty broad—and it's service for both partners; it's a two-way street.

The challenge, then, is to be a Master with good judgment and good leadership skills who is seen to be worthy of such service. The challenge, then, is to be a slave who has mastered a wide range of service skills that are put at Master's disposal.

—Robert J. (Dr. Bob) Rubel

What do you want from a relationship?

What is your *purpose* in entering into a Master/slave relationship? As a Master, do you have a desire to totally take care of someone, to be responsible for their mental, physical, emotional health? To be responsible for their education, their spiritual training, what they read and how they speak? Are you an established leader in your work life so all this will flow naturally to you, or do you need to get some training yourself in order to be a responsible Master?

If you're the slave, why are you considering surrendering authority over yourself to someone else? Do you prefer to be guided in your life decisions? Do you prefer the #2 slot in other parts of your life? Do you enjoy supporting someone that you believe in? What other benefits occur to you?

The late Jack McGeorge proposed that the purpose of an M/s dynamic is to achieve "an enduring relationship between a Master and slave who are worthy of each other." He went on to define worthy as: "Someone whose contribution to your life is commensurate with your efforts on their behalf; someone you are proud to call your Master or your slave; someone who strives to excel in their role." (Master Jack McGeorge's Handout for presentation at Southwest Leather Conference 2005: *Finding a Worthy Master or slave*.)

I certainly agree with Master Jack, and to flesh out his words, I propose a refining question: What kind of Master (or what kind of slave) are you thinking you'll be? Remember: you're creating a new kind of relationship model largely out of thin air. If you've never been involved in a structured relationship before, then this is all new to you. If you have been in a structured relationship before, then you realize that Master makes the rules and slave supports/follows those rules.

> Are you the kind of Master that you would serve?
>
> —M. Jen Fairfield

Interestingly, the rules can be that Master is serving as protector for his or her very creative slave and that it is the slave, more than the Master, who is the creative star of the team.

Let me take you on a little side-trip for a minute; I'd like to approach this topic a little differently.

How did you prepare for your profession? Did you have to go to school and learn stuff? Did you have to pass certifying examinations? Did you have to get a license?

Now: how did you prepare to be a good boyfriend or girlfriend when you were in high school or college… or beyond? Nothing, right? How did that work for you?

So, now you're considering entering into a completely new kind of relationship. Not only are you venturing into BDSM sexual play that requires you to learn new physical and mental skills, but you're changing the way you relate to your partner. That's a lot of new material to work with.

That's why a little introspection can be useful.

So let's get started…

At the risk of proposing polar extremes, consider some of these:
- Do you seek a servant to follow all your orders and whims or do you seek a cherished partner who expresses love through service?
- Do you seek a live-in sex object or do you seek a spiritual partner with whom you have hot sex?
- Do you seek an invisible chef and maid or a personal assistant with privileges?

Hazy goals produce hazy results. Clearly define your goals. Write them down, make a plan for achieving them, set a deadline, visualize the results, and go after them. Doubtless you've heard the aphorism: *What gets written down gets done.*

When reading this book in draft form, my friend Dan (AngelRiot on Fet) added: "I understand this side of the coin, that you'll never get where you want to be if you don't define where you want to be. But there is wisdom also in adapting to the opportunities that already exist in your life. I think only half of *life satisfaction* is found by achieving what you believe you want; the other half comes from appreciating what you have already achieved."

What kind of *life* or *lifestyle* do you seek?

You are going to have to tease out the building blocks of this kind of structured relationship. While you can certainly *drift* into a Master/slave relationship, *drifting* through life does not sound like the actions of a Master. It doesn't even sound like the actions of the kind of person a Master would want as a partner. My own mental image of a Master/slave couple is that of two people who want to design their lives purposefully and

Vision without action is a daydream. Action without vision is a nightmare.

—Japanese proverb

with intention and who have found that an authority-imbalanced relationship model serves their own needs. People on this path are not, in my experiences, the types of folks who go along in life just for the ride. That brings us to a question:

- In life, are you *proactive* or *reactive*? If you tend to be *reactive*, then what consequences might that have for your structured relationship?
- Have you written down your goals for the next five or ten years? How does a Master or slave (or two) fit into that vision? For example, if your vision is to live in a beautiful mountain cabin overlooking a lake and far away from a city, how does that mesh with your potential partner's thirst for big-city living, nice restaurants and theater?
- How's your imagination? Can you *think outside of the box*? Do you tend to be seen as someone who has both feet firmly planted on the ground, or are you a creative risk-taker? Do you have experience taking your vision and moving it to reality? (If the answer is "no," then you may want to consider books/courses that can train you in this art form. Hint: it has to do with *clarity of purpose* and *intent*. The key question is: "What are you willing to pay to get X result?" I'll be going into this in more details in about a dozen pages. Just keep this in mind, though: there's a *cost* to recreating yourself.)
- Do you read much? Fiction? Non-fiction? What do you do with

your knowledge? That is, do you keep knowledge to yourself or do you have a way of giving back to your community?

- Can you translate your ideas into words? How can you communicate your vision to your partner?

What kind of PERSON do you seek?

How clearly can you describe your fantasy partner? If you can't describe this person, how will you know when you find them?

_____

"When I examine myself and my methods of thought, I come to the conclusion that the gift of fantasy has meant more to me than my talent for absorbing positive knowledge."

—Albert Einstein

_____

- As a Master, what are you seeking in a partner? If the person is not a vanilla boyfriend or girlfriend, what IS your person to be??? Pleasure slave (sexual play partner)? Service slave (servant)? Business slave (Personal Assistant)? Companion/lover?
- As an s-type, what are you looking for in a partner? Do you understand the differences between a Dom and a Master? If you are looking for a Master, what kind of Master? Companion for their future? A sage/teacher/mentor to rely upon? A path for sexual release linked with some form of spirituality? Financial and/or emotional security? A life-travel buddy? A spiritual guide? Leather? Why?
- Does _what you offer_ match _what your potential partner seeks_? Financial or emotional stability? Sense of purpose? Adventure? Great sex?
- For you Masters… how are your assets? Can you afford to remake your slave (or slave-under-consideration) in your image?
- How smart, lucid, and articulate must your partner be? Does _quickness_ matter to you? Does it matter that your partner can explain him/herself succinctly and with precision and clarity?

Speaking personally, *quickness* matters a great deal to me. So does vocabulary level. IQ primarily helps people get quickly to answers—it's a *crunching power* issue. In that light, it may be reasonable for you to be concerned about IQ because the intellectual demands you can make on someone with an IQ of 100 will be different than you can make on someone with an IQ of 135.

- Do you want to have *shared values* with this person? Rather than a general *yes*, let's explore...

I would propose that at some point in your relationship you sit down with your partner—or partner-to-be—and probe how each of you feels about words that describe values. You might want to create a values list—very much like a pre-play negotiations checklist. Consider it a *pre-structured relationship* checklist. And there are no right or wrong answers. For example, your own values concerning biological family or orderliness may be substantially different from those of your partner. That is simply information. Discussing these points will probably help each of you to understand the other's reactions on such specific points.

Here is the start of a list to consider. You will have to find longer lists from which to create your own list, this is just a starting point for thinking about values. An Internet search produces dozens of exhaustive lists from which to work.

Accuracy	Discipline	Harmony with others
Adventure	Efficiency	Honesty
Beauty	Excellence of work quality	Honor, honor code
Cleanliness, orderliness	Fairness	Independence
Community	Faith, spirituality	Inner peace, calm
Competence	Family	Justice, fair play

Concern for others	Feelings, emotions	Innovation
Cooperation— team spirit	Fun, happy, lighthearted	Integrity
Coordination	Global view of life	Knowledge
Decisiveness	Hard worker	Leadership

Once again—the goal, here, is to take each word on this (and your expanded) list and discuss it with your partner in order to learn more about their (and your) basic beliefs. Since basic beliefs color your everyday reality, the more you know about yourself and your partner, the better you'll be able to work together harmoniously. Actually, in my own experience, it will help you a great deal to come to a common understanding of what each word means before you try to discuss the word's importance in each of your worlds. Also, it's tremendously helpful to place a value on each word. For example, you might assign a value of 1 to values that are somewhat important and a value of 5 for values that represent an aspect of your core belief system.

I'd like to insert a note that Dan (Fet=AngelRiot) brought up after he read this book in draft form: "Perhaps the most useful traits in a partner are empathy, willingness to adapt, and relationship tenacity." I agree.

What WON'T you accept?
This brings up the question about knowing what you *won't* accept in a relationship; knowing what does not serve you and your future.

Topics in this arena are intended to be viewed in two ways: first, as part of the screening process one person would go through when considering any potential partner; and second, a nudge to look at your OWN behavior—whether or not you are in an established relationship—in terms of your own flexibility and likeability. Like tends to attract like, so your own behaviors and mannerisms are part of the attraction others will feel towards you.

Some areas of personal behavior affect one's willingness to start or to maintain an intense authority-based relationship. I'd take this one step further:

I will skip the really obvious *character flaw* issues (dishonest, untrustworthy, etc.) and touch only on a few of the more subtle topics.

Personal habits: A bit too messy? Compulsively clean? How are your table manners? These are the little things that can wear on a partner. For example, if you open a kitchen drawer and see things stuffed in there, do you care? Does it matter to you whether the spice bottles in the kitchen are in alphabetical order with the labels facing outward? What about the orderliness of your closet—or your partner's side of the closet? What about your underwear drawer (socks folded?) or your partner's bedside table?

Personal preferences can range from the macro to the micro: from the city/state/country you'll live in to whether or not Master requires all electrical cords and cables to be laced (rather than piled in a tangle). But, Master's micro-level preferences can be a two-edged sword. On the one hand, Master may have baseline standards of neatness that the slave simply **will** adhere to; on the other hand, Master has to appreciate when his/her own preferences get in the way of the relationship, itself.

Which actually brings up a core concept in M/s dynamics that Raven Kaldera has mentioned in a workshop: Master is responsible for slave's "**can'ts** but slave is responsible for slave's **won'ts**." That is—Master is responsible for providing the necessary training and guidance so that slave can do whatever Master wishes, however only the slave can choose whether or not to comply with Master's wishes. By the way, this is where *passive-aggressive resistance* can come into play. Slave may test Master's leadership by superficially agreeing to do what Master wishes but—in actuality—largely ignoring Master's guidance in some areas.

Personal presentation—grooming and dress: One dresses (or, at least one should dress) in a manner intended to attract someone who would dress similarly. If you're looking for someone who likes to hang out at shopping malls, then blue jeans are your ticket. If you're looking for someone who likes to hang out at a four-star hotel lobby, then blue jeans are **not** your ticket.

I knew someone in a D/s relationship with a female submissive who (he said) would ONLY wear black and would ONLY wear spike heels when in public. Hard limits. Deal breakers. It was one of the first things she negotiated with him. Sound silly or inconsequential? That depends upon your personal lifestyle. Yes, the girl was stunning—a real Barbie. She definitely turns heads. But, there are situations in life where wearing spiked heels and dressing entirely in black makes you really, really stand out—and not in a good way. Think *wedding*, or *seaside resort*, or *summertime in Glacier Park at the elegant lodge for dinner.*

Can you live with this or something similar?

Let's turn the tables: I know a really prominent Dom in our local BDSM community who insists that *nobody* can tell him how to dress. I've seen him show up in blue jeans at a formal dinner party where everyone else was in fetish costuming. You can draw your own conclusions.

Correct use of English: In the same way that one dresses in a manner to attract a partner with similar tastes, the way you speak telegraphs your background—and that will be tied to a number of compatibility issues. I started life as a high school English teacher. When I hear someone using regional grammar (*I'd like **for** you to go to the market, please.*), I notice it. If someone uses incorrect English (*Jim **ain't** got a chance of making that shot.*), I notice it. If someone uses the wrong word (*Please keep me **appraised** of the situation.*), I notice it. And I will say, personally, that precise English and a large vocabulary are two of my own requirement for a potential partner.

Social manners/poise/personal mannerisms: Do you notice if a person wipes their mouth with a linen table napkin or pats their mouth? Do you care if a person (of either gender) plops down in a chair or couch, rather than lowering him/herself into place? Do you notice whether women cross their ankles when seated or cross their legs? Do you notice whether a woman is wearing hose with her sandals? What images are YOU projecting that would attract a person with the type of social manners that you seek? And before you jump in and say that this doesn't apply to you, mentally transport yourself to some extreme subculture—Borneo tribe, or inner-city ghetto, or elite country club in Beverly Hills. Your personal mannerisms mark you as part of or *not* part of that community. And some of these mannerisms are really subtle. For example, in world cultures, only American men put one leg across their other knee in a figure-4 style.

Sexual aptitude, appetite, and preferences: Are you a match or mismatch? In the early flush of a relationship, one is inclined to overlook some issues. "I wish she dressed up a bit more," or "I wish he didn't slurp his coffee," or "I wish she wouldn't drive so fast." While issues such as these can be handled through protocols within the context of an M/s relationship, the same is not true for sex. If one partner's idea of sex is five minutes of rolling around on the floor wrestling and fucking and the other person's idea is a two-hour sensual marathon, there's bound to be a problem—and it may not be very resolvable. If one partner is extremely sexually experienced and the other partner is not, there's bound to be a problem—and again, it may not be very resolvable, even with communication and counseling.

The problem with resolving sexual compatibility issues is that we're not taught much about how to coach people in this arena. So, women fake orgasms and men resort to finding other ways of feeling fulfilled. For those of us who live in the world of BDSM play, issues of sexual compatibility become even more complicated. What if your slave needs to be spanked/caned/flogged to get warmed up before serious rough sex that involves face slapping, but **your** ideal evening consists of spending an hour or so tying up your slave in an elaborate Shibari rope harness and then just sitting there watching him/her twist slowly from the suspension rig?

And what is sex for you, anyway? I have a friend for whom sex is fisting a woman without using lube—just saliva. He loves to hear her scream. It turns him on, and it is an important part of their sexual dance; he claims that he prefers it to penile penetration. If I hadn't watched it, I wouldn't have believed it. Safe? Nope. Did I say anything? Nope. My point, here, is that because we're kinky, we may have unusual sexual practices that require searching for that *special someone* in order to get our needs fulfilled. And because of this, you have to decide whether your partner's sexual preferences fall into the, "Oh, I don't think so" category, or—being ever creative—you want to maintain the M/s relationship with this person, but bring in a third for some of the specialized sexual stuff.

What is a *Master,* what is a *slave?*
Here's the question: Do you both agree about the roles and expectations of your respective positions?
- Does the slave clearly understand the Master's views (fantasies/hopes) of their role?
- Has the Master signed up to be the version of a Master that the slave dreams about at night?

In my experience, there can be a big (and often eye-opening) difference between the public fantasy "Me Tarzan—you jane" version of Master/slave relationships and the sophisticated and complex reality that is seen in established long-term relationships. Part of the challenge to understand one another's roles is that roles such as *Master* and *slave* or *dominant* and *submissive* don't have commonly accepted definitions. That is, while we all clearly understand what a *mommy* or *daddy* should be, that is not true when it comes to trying to understand what a *Master* or a *slave* should be.

There are no generally accepted standards of behavior, no standards for anchoring expectations. Even though you and your partner seem to be getting along well enough, but underneath it all, there is a risk that each has made some assumptions about the depth or breadth of their relationship that have not been explicitly discussed. That's risky.

It's risky when core values or basic assumptions differ between partners. When words such as *Master* or *submissive* (or other concept words) form the basis of a relationship, it's helpful when both partners are clear about their role expectations—not only about one another but about each other through the eyes of the other. It's easy to understand that once the two of you have sat down and discussed one another's personal values, traits, dreams, wants, and needs, you'll be in a much better position to be supportive and understanding. Fewer surprises.

The risk in NOT working through this exercise is that each of you may have been attracted to the superficial representation of the other person—you've been drawn to your partner's public face, rather than to the person's core being. While that may not be a bad thing, it may lead you to have to re-evaluate and re-adjust your on-going relationship more than you had initially expected.

While hardly an exhaustive list, here are some ideas about what a Master candidate might look like to a slave-in-waiting:

- Someone who understands that an M/s relationship is between **equals**—that the slave has no less value as a person than Master.
- A person who admits their personal weaknesses and is committed to turning those weaknesses into strengths and to continuing to develop emotionally and spiritually.
- Someone emotionally, physically, and intellectually equal to or stronger than the slave.
- Someone to be **responsible** for the slave's wellbeing and who considers the relationship above all else when making plans for the future.
- A person who has enough life experience, knowledge, and wisdom to serve as a mentor and teacher.
- A person who will hold the slave accountable to **high standards**. This includes a Master who is spiritually awake and uses the M/s relationship to further mutual spiritual development.
- A person who establishes an atmosphere of **safety**, even as he/she must discipline the slave for transgressions.
- A high-level communicator who maintains well-defined boundaries regarding **accepted** behavior.
- Someone who will be **honest,** even when knowing that the slave's reaction to the truth might be negative.
- A person who can demonstrate their understanding of the gift of service and obedience that is offered through the slave's submission.

Here are some ideas about what a slave candidate might look like to a Master. Again, this is just a starting point. You have to make your own list.

- A person experienced in the Leather culture, who understands the nuances of a structured relationship. Again, the fantasy of living 24/7 in a structured relationship is certainly different from the fantasies described in books such as, *The Marketplace* series.

- **A quick learner**. Someone who is likely to be adaptable to new situations. Someone who can apply knowledge to behavior. This describes a person in control of him/herself—not a person over-controlled by prior experiences. Let's face it; we all have baggage. Some people hang on to their baggage more than others. It's important when exploring an M/s relationship that the slave has the capacity to meld their world to the likes/dislikes of Master independent of the slave's own historical likes/dislikes. This takes flexibility.

- An **adventuresome** person who is committed to supporting you and your endeavors, regardless of where they lead.

- A person of **high moral/ethical behavior** who is also a clear communicator. This person must have the moral courage and integrity to be able to point out to Master behaviors that concerns the slave.

- Someone who has **experience serving others** and who demonstrates empathy and nurturing skills.

- Someone who **looks for the positives** in every situation. This person can be described variously as a *glass half-full* person or a *towards* person rather than an *away-from* person.

    Let me explain this one. In a general way, people tend either to reach towards new experiences or to react by turning away from new experiences. Some people embrace change, some resist change. Often, you will find that a litigating attorney is a *towards* person, but a contracts attorney is an *away from* person. That is, the litigator is trying to *obtain* (move towards) a victory for their client, but a contracts attorney is trying to keep their client away from (out of) trouble. For similar reasons, accountants also tend to be *away from* people—their natural inclination is to keep their clients from getting in trouble in some way. In business, *away from* people are concerned about protecting their client's interests or their own business position. In business, *towards* people are often found to be the visionary leaders.

When you put two *away from* people together, they tend to avoid risk-taking and—consequently—may not have many adventures. When you put two *towards* people together, they may engage in very exciting, but also very risky, behavior. Which brings us to the next bullet:

- Someone with **well-defined boundaries;** someone who is clear about establishing boundaries. Combining this idea with the idea discussed in the previous bullet, you can imagine two visionaries who are always out seeking new sensations and experiences, yet, who do this carefully and with appropriate discretion. Similarly, you can imagine two visionaries with poor boundary-setting skills that are so edgy that it makes others uncomfortable to be around them.
- A person with **wide-ranging skills in personal service**, plus, what I call, courtesan skills. These are skills of dressing well, music, dance, discourse, oral recitation and conversation. Among the personal service skills I would include high-level *executive assistant* skills: the ability to manage a small business, the ability to represent Master in professional settings, and so forth.

If your potential s-type is new to the Lifestyle—and if YOU are fairly new to the Lifestyle—your greatest risk probably lies in scaring him/her. I have a friend—a Leatherwoman who had been in the Lifestyle for a little over one year—who took a fairly new-to-the-lifestyle date to a "dark party" (a no-rules party), and was upset that he didn't know how to behave. Are we surprised, here?

I have another friend who was so excited about finally collaring his slave that he ordered her to wear the collar to work. Not a good idea; this collar wasn't very discreet. Soon, the slave's work life was embroiled in one minor controversy after another. The slave never lost her job, but she had the sense that she was monitored much more closely, and *differently*, than her peers—and her workload increased.

Message: it's going to take some time for those new to this subculture—whether new as a Master or new as a slave—to learn how to behave and act separately and together in ways that don't cause others to roll their eyes. How many times have we heard stories of Internet Doms showing up at a public play party and causing an uproar by grabbing someone's slave/submissive by the collar? How many times have we heard about the new person walking right across an ongoing scene? How many times have we watched with some mixture of horror and fascination as a new-to-real-life Dom would sit down beside someone's collared slave and start talking to her?

Anyway, the reality is that we all started out at the beginning, and once we've been submerged in this Lifestyle for some years, we tend to forget how different we are now from the person we were then. In my experience, the further I travel down the BDSM and M/s paths, the less I have in common with vanillas. I must be actively careful about what I say around (or what I expect from) vanillas.

Another message: Don't overwhelm your new slave candidate.

Chapter 5
Negotiations, Contracts, Collars, and Protocols

This chapter focuses on contracts and their relatives: collars and protocols.

Contracts can be controversial in the M/s world. They require thoughtfulness combined with introspection and empathy—and those skills take some time to acquire. As a result, new Masters with new slaves (those who would most benefit from contracts), often try to rely on what they consider to be their innate dominance and prior life-skills to manage the situation.

Some potential Masters don't seem to want the accountability that a contract requires. Some potential Masters seem to be intellectually lazy and avoid taking the time and trouble to work through the terms and conditions of their unfolding relationship. Some simply don't understand the mutual advantages to creating a contract—to mutually agreeing on what in the world each person expects of the other for the next X-number of months/years.

As I've mentioned elsewhere in this book: I'm 70; I've been heavily involved in the M/s world for over a decade; I have lots of experience in marriages and businesses: if you're recently starting out in an authority-imbalanced relationship, you're going to want a contract.

Done correctly, contracts align expectations, save emotional hurt, save anger, and they can often prevent reputations from getting damaged when a relationship ends up on the he-said/she-said rocks of dissolution.

In life, one gets what one asks for. Unlike a D/s setting, in an M/s structure the slave is often surrendering authority over themselves to someone they really don't know very well.

M/s structured relationships differ in many ways from vanilla relationships. One important difference is that you have the opportunity to discuss and negotiate a number of key issues up-front. These issues become the basis of our contract.

- How do each of your describe your respective roles and responsibilities? What style of leadership will Master use? What style of Master and what kind of slave? (Resource: *Paradigms of Power: Styles of Master/Slave Relationships* edited by Raven Kaldera.)
- How will each of you interact under stress… what are your communication triggers? How will you deescalate interpersonal psychological trauma?
- Do you have a mediator identified to help when the two of you seem locked down over some issue? (Sooner or later you're going to need someone to act as a mediator: trust me on this.)
- How do priorities concerning each person's biological family fit into the priorities of Master and slave?
- And on, and on, and on…

Contracts are not one-sided; they evolve out of discussions about each person's expectations concerning your unique dynamic. Contracts are a communication tool at the front end of the relationship. Master does not create and present a contract TO the potential slave. Done correctly, contracts (and protocol books) go a long way towards smoothing out areas of potential discord between people. Interestingly, the more prior relationships you've had—particularly those involving marriage— the more useful a contract can be. Consider it to be a kinky pre-nuptial agreement.

This chapter may sound familiar if you've previously read my book: *BDSM Mastery—Relationships: a guide for creating mindful relationships for Dominants and submissives*. That version is tailored to a D/s relationship; this version is tailored to an M/s relationship.

So: here we go.

In structured relationships, there commonly are two types of documents, a Contract and a Protocol Manual. These are parallel to Articles of Incorporation and By-Laws for corporations: in our form of government, they are parallel to the Constitution and the Bill of Rights.

While a BDSM contract will set forth the overall structure of the House—the terms, conditions, and values of the key players—a *Protocol Manual* will be person- and position-specific. That is, one Master may have a slave serving as a Personal Assistant and a different slave serving as Household Manager. We'll touch on protocols later in this chapter. Here, I'm only concerned with the contract phase of the relationship, for the relationship has to be in place for some time before you can develop a sense of the personal protocols that you'll want used by your slave.

Before you Negotiate

This section highlights negative characteristics people exhibit that should be considered before you get too far involved with someone to be able gracefully to back out. Since I've covered this material in great detail in the book: *BDSM Mastery—Basics: your guide to play, parties, and scene protocols* and don't want to repeat all of it here. For those of you who have not read that book, this is a brief summary.

≠≠≠≠≠≠≠≠≠≠≠≠≠≠≠≠≠≠≠≠≠≠≠≠≠≠≠≠≠≠≠

While one should certainly endeavor to see good in all people and situations (silver lining, and all that), you have a responsibility to yourself and those who love you not to be overly gullible. I've assembled a few of the more critical areas where you may want to exhibit particular care and caution.

General cautions about people

Everyone is human. We all have foibles and follies. But, if you've run into someone who is exhibiting a number of the following traits, chances are that person is *miserable* with him or herself. Someone who is personally miserable is really likely to make YOU miserable. So tread carefully; be very careful with a person who:

- uses "I" as often as possible;
- is sensitive to (perceived) slights by others;
- is jealous and envious;
- thinks primarily of him/herself;
- talks mainly of him/herself;
- trusts no one;
- never seems to forget a criticism;
- always expects to be appreciated, always fishing for compliments;
- is suspicious of the intentions of others;
- listens greedily to what others say of him/her;
- frequently mentions faults in others;
- does as little as possible for others;
- shirks duties, if possible;
- never forgets a service he/she may have rendered to someone;
- sulks if people aren't grateful for their favors;
- demands agreement with their own views on everything;
- always looking for a good time;
- loves him/herself first; or
- is selfish, if at all possible.

So, whether you're looking for a Master or a slave, remember the aphorism: There's always free cheese in a mousetrap.

Now, most people are pretty sure that they're okay. Most people think that most others are also pretty much okay. But, some people think that certain people are **not** okay. The thing of it is, the person who *you think is not so okay* probably thinks he's just fine. So, let me explore this a little.

Our Community—and here I'm combining the Leather and the not-Leather BDSM Communities—contains mostly bright, dynamic and interesting people. It also contains some really average people.

And, too, it contains some icky people. As I just mentioned, **they** probably won't think of themselves as presenting problems within the Community, but others do. To describe these folks, Jay Wiseman coined the phrase: *Poor Quality Dominants* (PQDs). I have also heard this topic discussed at Leather Leadership conferences. Consider whether you know someone with these characteristics:

Disclaimers:
- When you label someone as a poor quality person (whether a D- or s-type), your decision must be based upon your own personal observations, not on hearsay. Beware of repeating gossip. Also, you need to consider what you will do if you're accused of traits such as these.
- No, I'm not thinking of any real person; but if you think I'm describing you, you may—in fact—have a problem.

While you'll certainly hear about predatory or "bad-acting" *men* much less seems to surface about bad-acting women, but you will find one or two within in our community. You'll find women who are do-me queens, drama-queens, emotional vampires, and financial predators. You'll not have a lot of fun in your relationship if you become entangled with someone who gossips, shares their troubles with you behind your back, or is deceptive about the *intent* about their relationship with you.

Here are some defenses that are helpful whether your intended is a D- or s-type:
- Ask your potential partner to provide references. References that you already know. This may be somewhat round-about, but it can be done. Person "X" knows person "Y," who knows person "Z," whom you also know. Ours is a pretty small Community.

- Do some additional research. Learn something about the person you are considering. Listen for what you are NOT being told, as well as what you ARE being told. Listen for unusual phrasing: "Oh, gosh, sure I know XYZ. Oh, I don't think it's appropriate for me to say anything about them—that would sound too much like gossip, you know what I mean?"

- Because our Community so relies on *personal endorsements*, it's *extremely important* that you couldn't get one for XYZ. Your follow-up question might be: "Oh, can you give me the name of anyone who *could* give me an endorsement?" If your source now says something like: "Oh, gosh, that would really be hard. I just don't know…" you know that you've just unfurled a big red flag.

- Attend your local kink meeting with your potential friend. How do they behave? Are they welcomed like a person of high value, or like some gruesome plague? Does this person appear to be surrounded by a closed circle of friends (a clique?), or does this person mix with the general assembly? In fact, what conclusions can you draw about this person by the others with whom they meet?

Relationship cautions for Masters and slaves

By the time you've been involved with BDSM long enough to be interested in forming a Master/slave relationship, you've already run into a buzz saw or two. When it comes to questionable D-type behavior, one imagines the person pushing limits, not respecting the s-type's needs, or sexually using a newbie s-type (who is emotionally off-balance because of the tremendously new and unusual experiences afforded by this lifestyle). When it comes to questionable s-type behavior one thinks of drama queens, financial predators, and emotionally broken people.

Here is a brief cautionary list to consider.

Hasn't done their homework: Your new partner has accepted this relationship with you, but has NOT checked YOUR reputation within your local BDSM community. If your potential partner hasn't checked you out, they may be unusually naïve or so new to the community that they don't know *how* to check you out. Or, they may be a little arrogant and feel that they can discern all your strengths and weaknesses on their own. This is not likely to be true, is it?

Have *issues* that are not easy to evaluate: Your new partner may be addicted to drugs, alcohol, sex, pain, food, etc. While active additions will be pretty self-evident, addictive behavior patterns can be hidden and/or misinterpreted by those not trained to recognize them. But, people with active or prior addictions have certain common characteristics that can include stunted emotional development—so, you may wish to do some research into *addictive behavior* before getting too heavily involved with our community. Anyway, it's a good piece of general knowledge to have.

Secretive: Your new partner won't account for a block of time that has disappeared. He/she keeps ducking and weaving when asked the simple question: "Where were you?" (Warning: she/he may have been out finding you a surprise birthday present—so, be careful about forcing an answer.)

Hidden behavior: The s-type keeps an online journal (blog) that you either don't know about or don't monitor on the grounds that it is trivial. (I know of a case where a Dom chose not to monitor his submissive's blog. As it happened, she was a disturbed person and was broadcasting extremely private and negative half-truths about him. These unchallenged fabrications went around the submissives' network like wildfire and caused him to be declared *persona non grata* in a number of local clubs.)

Drama-prone: Your new slave has frequent personal crises beyond the normal or average that could be expected in any life. This could indicate that this person may—through their personal choices—bring these problems upon themselves. I doubt that you will enjoy being along for that ride.

Moody: Your new partner seems to have dramatic mood swings: nice and pleasant most of the time, then aggressive and abusive without warning. Same comment as above: this is not normal and you will probably not want to get involved.

Passive/aggressive behavior: He/she keeps saying, "Yes," yet your request is ignored or poorly completed. Outward behaviors such as these have deep roots. It's not likely you will be able to do something with a fully-grown adult who exhibits them.

Warnings from others: People seem to be trying to tell you something about your slave candidate, but you can't quite understand what they're getting at. You sense that you're being offered a warning, but you bristle, and the other person retreats. All I can say to this is: suppress your knee-jerk defense of the slave candidate and listen.

Refusal to negotiate: Your slave-to-be doesn't want to have a formal negotiation and contract with you on the grounds that this is a Master/slave relationship, and as Master, you surely know how to treat him/her, and you only need to know that he/she wants to serve you. Ummmm, errrrr this is, perhaps, an Internet person? Knowing, understanding, and communicating your limits and needs will help prevent abuses of trust.

Community-wide cautions

Beyond concerns that affect individuals in a relationship, there is a deeper level of concern about people—usually male dominants—that often infects a community. I've assembled this list of cautions just to remind you of some lessons you've probably already learned. When you find people like these, you'll probably not want to become overly friendly.

Speaks ill of others: The person is quick to categorize other Doms in his Community as, *Poor Quality Dominants*, and he works to isolate them. (That is, the very fact that he categorizes people this way should be a red flag about *his own* attitudes and actions. Sure, there may actually be a few people in the Community who genuinely cause trouble—but, they are rare and will be broadly recognized for what they are within the Community.) This type of person speaks ill of others as a *preemptive strike*, **assuming** the other person (people) will tell the truth about him.

Spreads malicious gossip: The person spends his energies spreading gossip that is negative about the good works of others within the Community, rather than creating his own works, projects, or organizations. If he does build his own organization, it's a sham: its real purpose is to have a vehicle that he can brag about as his own, rather than as a positive force in the Community. He may be known for trying to take over another organization after being (at last) cast out of the previous one.

Tries to dominate other Doms: The person tends to try to dominate other Doms. He finds that he has a little clique of "warriors" around him who are quick to exclude others from his group. He tends to feel that his way is the right way and that other ways are less than his correct way.

Won't listen to advice: The person declines to take counsel from Seniors—those who have been in the scene a long time—because he consider himself to be a Senior, and thus, doesn't have to listen to anyone.

Legend in his own mind: The person engages in self-aggrandizement. He takes credit where credit is **not** due. He claims to have started an organization, but he didn't. He starts calling himself Master XYZ—but no Senior Leather Master will respect that self-appointed title. He bought his own Master's cap.

My way or… The person has a tendency to take his ball and walk off the court if he can't control a group or a situation. Closely allied: people around him feel that they must do things his way or it's the highway. He mostly cooperates in situations that benefit him.

Few friends: The person has a very small and tight-knit circle of friends who seem not to last very long. He constantly throws people out of his inner circle for various reasons. He has a string of former friends who cross the street to avoid him. If he wanted to give a party, his first thought wouldn't be "Gosh, where can I find a place big enough?" it would it be "Gosh, who would I want to spend the evening with?" or (worse yet) "Who would want to spend the evening with **me**?"

Attracts controversy: The person finds himself repeatedly embroiled in some local controversy or flare-up—often on an e-group.

The message, here, is that while some people may exhibit one or two of the characteristics in this list (yes, I'm being charitable), if you know someone with many of these characteristics, then this person may not be very in touch with what others within the Community think of him. He may have something of a tainted reputation and not really know it. Interestingly, it's been my repeated experience that people who exhibit a number of these characteristics have such thorough psychological barriers to meaningful self-examination that they have elaborate ways to explain and justify the controversies they cause. They see their lack of friends and their difficulty in finding or keeping a slave as being a problem/flaw in *others*. Attempts to aid and counsel people with these kinds of blinders will only get you cast out along with the others from their past. Typically, these are very, very angry people.

So, did you recoil at this list? That's okay. I put it here so you could be aware of these and similar traits when it comes to selecting a slave or a Master. You need to find out your candidate's track record. You need to do some research into the congruency between what the person *says*, and what the person *does*.

Negotiations

Contracts result from negotiations. They are not pulled off the Web; they are not borrowed from Master X down the street. Contracts give Master the opportunity to say: "Look, this is what I believe in, this is what I'm concerned about, this is how I'd like you to interact with me… okay?" Contracts give the potential slave the opportunity to foresee not only what Master values but also areas where there may be potential conflict. If you don't understand something, ask: "With respect, Master, I'm not sure I fully understand this section. Can we discuss this?" or "Master, with respect, I understand that I'll be in service to you 24/7, but this slave wonders what provisions Master is considering to provide this slave with time to manage its own emails and personal obligations?" or "Master, with respect, this slave doesn't see anything in this Contract relating to helping it to develop an emotional support group not only for itself, but to turn to in the case that either of us has a medical emergency."

For contracts to work, they must be real. For the initial training contract to work, it has to be fairly simple and non-threatening.

Note to Masters: This person may not know you very well (or may be junior to you in the lifestyle), so the very fact that you're presenting them with a contract may be intimidating. The longer and more complex the contract, the more likely they'll be cautious about it. The more the contract specifies what *they* will do for you and the less you include about what you will do for *them*, the more likely they'll be cautious about it.

As I've said before, for many of us in this community, *ownership* is the dividing line between Dom/me and Master, submissive and slave: while a Dom/me has **influence** over their submissive, a Master has **authority** over their slave. This is why D/s relationships are based in *power exchange* and are generally scene-specific, while M/s relationships based on *authority transfer* and represents an absolute and ongoing commitment to Master's authority.

Master's authority stems from ownership. For Master to own a slave, that person (wherever they fall on the scale of dominance or submissiveness) must surrender their own authority over themselves to the absolute authority of their Master's will. Among other things, that means that the slave-to-be has to agree that slave is no longer a person in their own right and is only what Master wishes it to be. The slave no longer has control over its own time, the planning for its own future, what it may or may not say to Master or to others, and what it is to learn in order to be in service to this Master. That's a lot to surrender—which is why M/s structures are so rare and require such careful construction.

The next few pages are about negotiating the ownership and use of your slave's soul.

Heady stuff.

For starters, unless you've been trained in negotiating styles and techniques, you'll want to read these sections more than once. Also, if you're negotiating with an intended slave who has not negotiated a number of prior contracts, moral/ethical honor binds you to recommend to your intended that he/she seek an experienced Master to represent him/her in negotiations with YOU.

Opening notes

In real-life business negotiations, it is a truism that the *real guts of the negotiation occur just as the clock is running out*. That is, if you allow an hour for a negotiation, most of the serious issues finally are resolved in the last five minutes. If you allow a day, they get resolved in the last five minutes. If you allow a week, they get resolved in the last five minutes.

Negotiations are resolved most quickly and cleanly if you understand your partner's needs/wants through their eyes. The better you understand what the *other person* **needs** (as opposed to what they say that they **want**), the cleaner and clearer the negotiation. That said, I'll now start in on this section.

≠≠≠≠≠≠≠≠≠≠≠≠≠≠≠≠≠≠≠≠≠≠≠≠≠≠≠≠≠≠≠

Much is said about negotiations. *Negotiations* live in the world of D/s (for scening) and M/s (for the first few years of the relationship, at any rate).

In my experience, a Dominant who is not used to business-level negotiations often starts to negotiate with a potential slave before doing any or much background research. In particular, they start negotiating what the potential slave will and will not be permitted before even spending a weekend alone with them. They don't know much about the person with whom they're negotiating. Sort of silly, in my view. (I once watched a "senior Dom" try to go down that path. He was informing her what she could and couldn't do and how she was to address him. He didn't realize that she was an equally senior and beautifully trained slave who was a slick negotiator in her own right. She blew him off as being an asshole. His loss, trust me. I was particularly astonished, as I knew that this Master had taught classes in contract negotiating at BDSM conferences.)

By the way, I caution you against drafting an extensive initial training contract that exposes your intended slave to the full brunt of your idiosyncratic fantasies and accompanying protocols: you're likely to trigger all their fears that you're seeking free maid and sex services while kowtowing to an autocratic bully. When preparing a contract, ask yourself: would YOU sign it?

Now, I certainly endorse the use of very simple short-term contracts that provide minimal guidance for both parties while the two people endeavor to learn about one another, but the goal of the contract would be to assure one another that the intent of your time together is to get to know one another. As with all aspects of life, the more you know about something, the better able you are to adapt/adjust to that *something*. Thinking of moving to Borneo? Chances are you'd do a lot of preparatory study about Borneo. Thinking of flying an airplane? Chances are you'd do a lot of preparatory study about flying. Thinking of taking on a slave or a Master?

- Consider putting yourself and your intended partner through a series of personality and skill-battery tests. At a minimum, an online IQ test and a Meyers-Briggs test; ideally, find some tests that will demonstrate both your preferred working styles (the Kolbe A exam) and your mutual skill preferences.

- Consider taking courses/workshops that promote a common set of problem solving skills—The Landmark Education Forum comes to mind. They also offer a 10-week communications course that I've gone through before marrying my second wife and, 17 or so years later, with my former Owner and slave before we all moved in together. Common language is a good idea. As the humorous saying goes: "After all, how many of us are speaking the same language even when we're speaking the same language?"

WHAT to Negotiate
For the sale of this book, I'm going to assume that you are going to start out with a *training contract*, and not a full-blown M/s contract stipulating your respective roles and responsibilities. A full-blown contract may very well scare away your potential slave. I strongly suggest that your first contract covers only the *getting-to-know-you* stage.

In a general way, I suggest you negotiate the *indicators of success for the next three months*. What does *success* look like to Master and to slave? What does *failure* look like? Note: the points I'll mention here live outside the boilerplate language of a contract. I'll assume that Master is agreeing to cherish slave and to train slave in various ways; I'll assume that slave is agreeing to serve with humility and to please Master in various ways, and so forth. These comments go beyond those statements/actions:

- If you're going to require the slave to be studying, what will they be studying and how much time does that involve per day or week?
- If the slave is going to be journaling, what is the content of the entries and how long must they be? (NOTE: I failed to negotiate this with my first slave! As a result, she thought that sending me summaries of her daily *activities* fulfilled her journaling obligations. I was looking for introspection and didn't care very much about what she did at work during the day. As a result, we were both disappointed about the journaling experience: she was hurt that I didn't respond to her writing; I was disappointed that I wasn't getting any meat—emotional content—out of the exercise.)
- If you are going to allow your slave to retain certain rights, be crystal clear about that. For example, at this early stage, will Master have authority over the slave's…
    - Contact with their biological family?
    - Use of money, including clothing purchases?
    - Hair/makeup style?
    - Workplace and work hours?
    - Academic and spiritual studies?
    - Weight and food choices?
- During this trial period, you may want total and solitary sexual access to your slave. But, there are many combinations out there. I know of a case where the slave is owned by someone who wanted to take her to swinging parties—and that had to be negotiated up front. I know another case where a woman had her own vanilla lover of many years before becoming a slave to another man. These special situations have to be addressed with care and sensitivity.

- Staying on the sexual front for a minute, will you, as Master, require the slave to stop all self-pleasuring during this period? And what if Master considers *self-pleasuring* to include eating chocolate? Again, be specific.
- How much responsibility are you agreeing to take on during this opening period? What if…
    - The slave is fired from work five weeks into the relationship and can't make their rent payment? Do you take over? (This happened to my first slave.)
    - The slave is out running an errand for you and is injured in a car accident; what is your moral/ethical position? What if it's YOUR car?
    - You are playing with your slave and you hit a *landmine* that brings up trauma to the point that he/she requires therapy. What's your moral/ethical position in *this* case?
- If you wish your slave to dress in a certain way, who is paying for the outfits during the trial period? Will you pay for the first $500 for outfits that please you? The first $200 or $1,500? (You may think I'm pulling this stuff out of thin air—I'm not. My fetish involves slave dressing elaborately for full fetish formal dinners. For me, a slave's appeal is affected by how she looks when *all dressed up*. Dressing this way extends to manicures, pedicures, and shoe choice, as well as hair and makeup combinations. This brings up the question: *What will you pay—in time and money—to make your relationship magical?*)
- What if **you** are an experienced player, but **your slave** is fairly new to the Lifestyle: are you still going to negotiate playing by RACK standards, or are you going to go back to SSC rules until your slave gains a greater level of trust with you? Does your slave understand the differences between SSC and RACK?
- If you are requiring a *full disclosure contract*, does your slave candidate fully understand what you mean by that phrase? You may want to explain clearly that this will mean that you can rightfully demand to know from your slave **anything** that another person says to him/her in confidence. Further, you should explain that your slave will be bound to volunteer that information to you if, in their heart-of-hearts, the slave knows that Master really should know about it. Jay Wiseman points

out that this creates a separate duty on the slave's part to tell someone *in advance* that nothing said to this slave can be held in confidence.

Too much work? Think you can bypass some of these minutiae? Maybe, maybe not. Did you ever consider what could happen if you don't go through a thorough negotiation process? Seen this one, lately? It's called *The Etiology of a Crisis*. I've added the M/s storyline.

- **Wild Enthusiasm:** Ohmygosh, I finally found someone willing to be my slave!!
- **Disillusionment:** Ohmygosh, this person is not such a good fit; how could I have done this???
- **Total Confusion:** Ohmygosh, I actually signed a three-month training contract with this person, and my word is my bond, and he/she's making me crazy.
- **Search for the Guilty:** This must be her fault. She must have hidden faults from me—everyone knows I'm an excellent judge of people.
- **Punishment of the Innocent:** Okay, I'll terminate our contract on the grounds that she won't obey me and then make up some reason why I can excuse myself for treating her as my enemy within the Community.
- **Promotion of the Uninvolved:** I'll go over here and take "X" as my new slave. This will show everyone who is watching that there's nothing wrong with ME.

Negotiating Wisely
Here are some general observations and rules about negotiating:
- We negotiate all the time; almost everything is negotiable.
- Avoid taking a position early in the discussion.
- First, create value. Why should someone want *you* or what you are offering?
- The first option isn't necessarily the best option. Create many options.
- Deadlines can be tricky when you're negotiating matters of the heart. (The general rule in business negotiations is to negotiate early or risk your opponent using deadlines—real or imagined—to trap you into conceding in their favor.)

- "No" means "no" when dealing with sexual issues. However, you may sometimes treat "no" as *not yet* if you're negotiating a service issue. Often "no" simply indicates that you haven't explained the benefits in terms that appeal to your listener.
- While the textbook on tough negotiations instructs you to give concessions only when you get something in return, you might consider introducing humorous concessions when you negotiate your M/s contract. That is, if Master wants the floors scrubbed each Saturday morning, the concession could be that Master takes his slave out to dinner each Saturday night. Remember, this is voluntary servitude and Master is responsible for the slave's mental well-being. Translation: slaves need time off.
- Use: "What if..." to break open the discussion to create value.
- You must leave the other person with a sense of satisfaction. This is the *win/win* school of negotiation, not the *winner takes all* school.
- Do your homework. Determine your partner's unexpressed needs. You'll need to probe. *Why* does your intended Master or slave seek certain specific terms or conditions.
- Using imagination, take the other person into the future to see possible results of various positions.

Negotiation challenges

Some negotiations go better than others, yes? Sometimes you come away feeling really good about the outcome, but sometimes you feel that the other person got more than you did. Here are some reasons.

Disparity of power: You may be exhibiting—or you may be negotiating with someone exhibiting—*Alpha male* characteristics: pushy, assertive, and aggressive. Apart from having to decide if you want this kind of personality in your life, you may find it nearly impossible to be heard during these negotiations. That's a problem that's not likely to go away any time soon. But, now you know some things about this person that they don't know you know: they're a bully and they don't know much about win/win negotiations. By extrapolation, they will most likely be using the, "Me Tarzan" model of M/s where Master is always right because they're Master.

Another power disparity comes into play during negotiations such as this if your opposite (either the Master looking for the slave or the slave looking for the Master) may need to sell themselves to you more than you need to add them to your life.

Disparity of information:
- Your opposite may have done much more research on you than you did on them.
- Your opposite may be *much more experienced* in M/s relations than you, and may **assume** that you know/understand things that never even occurred to you.
- The other person may specifically be *hiding things from you* and purposefully leave them out of the negotiation.
- Your opposite may know that he/she has another candidate in the wings if you don't work out. In the alternative, they may suspect/know YOU have another candidate waiting, if they don't work out.

Disparity of experience: You may have this kind of interview/ negotiation all the time; your opposite may do it only once or twice a year. This is particularly true of men who are negotiators in work settings, and also of Dominants who may be more used to interviewing or negotiating with subs for BDSM scenes or for relationship positions.

Along a similar line of thought, the slave candidate may not be used to thinking like a salesman, yet the success of this negotiation depends upon each of you selling yourselves to the other.

Disparity of pressure: Are you rushing in to replace a relationship that just ended? Are you under social or personal pressure to demonstrate that you're okay and the proof is that you can immediately form another relationship?

Hmmm. Lots to think about.

Let me offer a quick recap. You're serious about starting a new relationship. You've decided that this potential partner is okay—no skeletons hiding in the closet—you've read about negotiations, and you're ready to put your first contract together.

Good going. You're right in here with me.

Contracts

I've heard people dismiss M/s contracts out-of-hand. Their argument is that because it's not possible to make a legally binding contract in the U.S. that gives enforceable control over one person to another person that therefore there is no point to it—that it is a waste of time.

I differ.

Strongly.

slave contracts, while having no standing in court, force the two of you to talk about and work through the most fundamental aspects of your proposed lives together. Even if you're both married to one another and are now converting your marriage to M/s, the contracting phases enables the two (or more) parties to sit down and work through relationship issues that often are *assumed* to be one way or another.

People tend to forget things; details wash away with time—and age. *Contracts don't change their minds*. This is not a trivial issue. A clearly worded contract helps prevent needless upsets and recriminations… "But you promised me…," "I never said any such thing…," "But I thought you meant…"

Why Write a Contract?!

Contracts are a record of what each of you were thinking (hoping for) when you started your relationship.

Contracts are a way of describing and clarifying the exchange of Master's guidance for slave's service.

In this book, I've included only one contract. I call it a "getting to know you" contract. Beyond that, I'll be sending you to a couple of Websites.

However, before you're ready for those, I'd like to discuss some of the common styles of contracts and some of the more common clauses you'll find in contracts of this kind. By now, you probably have one eyebrow cocked and are reflecting on my opening aphorism: When *you don't know what to do, do it slowly.* Yes, this entire process takes a while.

Types of contracts

Let me start out by saying that contracts are best used by those who are either just starting their Master/slave relationship or have lived together without a contract and sense that they need to bring a little structure and organization to their lives to keep the dynamic fresh and real. In a general way, once you've become an established and stable couple (or more), the contract becomes more of a verbal pledge: Master pledges to serve the relationship and ensure that slave's needs are met; slave pledges to serve, honor, and obey Master.

But, let me start at the beginning. Let's say you are, in fact, going to prepare a document that specifies the contractual obligations of the partners, better to understand the proposed authority transfer relationship. There are three main ways to consider doing this that have worked for other people. I'm sure that there are other ways to do it, but these are the more common ways of approaching contracts in the M/s Lifestyle.

Time-controlled contract: This defines the obligations and duties each will assume at certain points along their agreed path. Normally, the defined level of authority transfer starts as a simple structured definition of the relationship at the time. The contract specifies the **furthest** level of authority transfer that is comfortable for both parties and explains commensurate duties and obligations. In between are a number of stages, normally between two and four, with each step mapped out.

The level of authority transfer is normally increased over time, though I am aware of one where the final stage was a required dissolution of the relationship. The timing of when the contractual stages come into force are not usually in the contract. Instead, it is up to the slave to inform the Master that he/she is ready for the next stage (thus giving consent), and for the Master then to inform the slave when the next stage will come into effect (thus retaining control).

This type of contract may be most applicable when two people are quite certain at the outset that their relationship will work out, and they know the path along which they wish to travel. While I've never known a couple to use this structure, it seems to me that this would be useful when Master is much more experienced than slave and is clear about where they wish to lead that slave over time.

Single stage (simple) contract: This contract lays out the core obligations and duties on both sides. This defines the balance of power or authority transfer at the time and leaves open any decrease or increase in that exchange. Typically, these contracts have no ending date. This contract is also known as a No Limits Contract and is usually used in an Owner/slave relationship, rather than a Master/slave relationship. Often, the exchange is thus:

- Master agrees to cherish and care for the slave and to always work for the slave's physical, mental, emotional, social, spiritual, and financial wellbeing.
- slave agrees to serve and to obey Master.

Several contracts used in stages: This type of contract may be more applicable when two people wish to begin exploring a path together. Here, Master may begin with some kind of temporary contract—perhaps a contract that covers a weekend, or a week or so. This can be viewed as a *getting to know you* contract. It may be fairly brief, but it gives each partner some starting points for developing their relationship.

Next, Master may offer a training contract that could last for a number of months, and could, perhaps, be renewed if Master didn't feel the slave had accomplished enough during the first contract period.

Following that, Master may offer a more extensive contract during a courting period—a period where Master is deciding whether to accept this slave for a lifetime commitment.

Finally, Master may offer the slave a much-simplified contract for life.

Some notes about contracts and re-upping: Each time one contract ends, the NEXT contract is negotiated and prepared. This is done so that both parties understand the level of authority transfer they must now meet, and also (as with the single time-controlled contract) understand the objective for the next stage, so they can strive to meet it.

A new *type* of contract is only created once Master is assured that the intent of the previous contract has been fulfilled; that the slave has been able to live within the power and authority structure described in the expiring contract.

Although it may be hard to accomplish, I strongly suggest that you let one contract expire, and use the next 4-6 weeks to negotiate the next staged contract from a position of *equal personal power*. That is, I urge you NOT to negotiate the next contract from within the M/s relationship. After all, if the slave has given the Master all authority over him/her, how in the world does the slave suddenly have the power to *negotiate*???

Common wording in contracts

A cautionary beginning: When I started reviewing online slave contracts, I was be struck by (actually, appalled by) the language giving the Master permission to punish and control the slave. In my experience, those who have chosen the path of *slave* view it as a *calling*. They are seeking to be recognized and cherished for doing a good job in their service—and *punishment for trivial issues* will drive them from the relationship.

NOTE: I realize that *domestic discipline* is a fetish—that many s-types are seeking a strong Master specifically to be caught and punished at every opportunity. That form of relationship is different from the M/s structure I'm describing in this book: in my world, that kind of behavior is a form of D/s fetish. Nothing wrong with it so long as both partners think it's a lot of fun, but M/s just isn't about having a license to punish your partner for less-than-perfect service. In my experience, a person on the path of *Internal Enslavement* (IE), or *Total Power Exchange* (TPE), is incredibly compliant to begin with.

Along this same line, I strongly urge you to consider that many of the slave contracts you'll find online stem from the porn version of Masters and slaves. In real life, you have a leader and a follower and each of you is just trying to get clear about what the other expects so that the two of you can live in peace and harmony.

There are many sample contracts available on the Internet. You may find it hard to identify a pre-existing contract that you could use—without alteration—in your own real-life relationship. That's because people (and their relationships) are so different. At any rate, when drawing up a personal contact, you might want to consider:

- **Key actors:** Who are each of you? What roles do you intend to play?
- **Exclusivity:** Are both of you single and unattached or are others to be involved in this relationship? If *others,* then go into detail describing everyone's role and responsibility.
- **Biological Family:** What provisions are made for any biological family members, especially minor children or aged parents?
- **Breadth of control:** Does this contract hold true outside the house or only at home? If it carries outside the house, where should you both agree that there are exceptions to the control agreed upon in this contract?
  - Slave's biological family
  - Professional/work life
  - Religious/spiritual training
  - Existing financial condition—savings/retirement accounts, future earnings, etc.
- **Outedness:** (I know it's not a word.) Are either of you *out* or still closeted? Will either of you be using a scene name? Does your biological family know about your lifestyle and relationship choices? How will you behave in public? How are you going to behave at your family's Holiday party?
- **Health:** Here, discuss issues of fluid bonding, sexually transmitted infections, safer-sex practices, and any mental health issues you know of. [NOTE: I recommend that you do NOT include any specific discussion of weight loss or exercise in your contract. However, you *can* mutually commit to the concept of maintaining some mutually agreed-upon fitness

standard. It makes much more sense for specific exercise requirements to be part of your Protocol Manual. Also, dietary and exercise requirements may change over time, but the Contract does *not* change over time.]

- **Mutual wants and needs:** Simply put—what does each party to this contract get out of signing it? What are the benefits to Master and to slave? Will the slave agree to cosmetic surgery? Will the slave agree to specialized training, such as attending a cooking or butlering academy? Might the slave be required to learn another language or move out of the US? Will the Master go through management or team training courses? Will the Master study communication and teaching strategies?

- **Property:** May the slave own property? May the slave bring property with it into the relationship? (As previously mentioned) who owns the slave's current assets and debts? Will finances now be shared or kept separate?

- **Speaking freely:** will the slave be permitted to speak freely to the Master? If yes, are there protocols that shield the slave from being punished for speaking freely? Does this contract recognize that the slave is honor-bound to notify the Master when the Master is about to do something that is seriously not-okay with the slave? Does this contract include provisions for slave to alert the Master to some serious issue/problem when in public without violating the authority imbalance? (This kind of material is covered in detail in my *Protocols* book.)

- **Punishment:** Will you distinguish between *punishment* and *correction*? Do you distinguish between *punishment* and *funishment*? Will you distinguish between *reactance* and *resistance*? Under what circumstances may the Master punish the slave? What will be involved in that punishment? Will there be release through atonement after the punishment?

- **Markings and piercings:** Will Master be permitted to mark slave? To have slave pierced or tattooed?

- **Safety:** What emotional and financial safeguards are you going to put in place for the slave, both during the relationship and upon demise of the relationship (or upon the untimely death of the Owner or the slave). What physical play safeword will you be using, *Red*? What emotional upset safeword will you be using, Master's given name?

- **Sexuality**: Does this contract include sex? If so, how is *sex* defined. Is it *intercourse* or is it *SM play* of some kind? Or something else? Is the Master free to play sexually with others? Is the slave equally free to play with others? Can the slave be loaned out? Will this be a multi-slave Household? This is the place to discuss any issues of polyamory, swinging, multiple slaves, and so forth. This is also the place to discuss sex with others of the same gender.
- **Openness**: Is the nature of the relationship to be discreet, or open and obvious to the public, work colleagues, family, etc.? Have you discussed *transparency?* Does Master recognize his/her own obligation to be transparent to the slave? Does the slave realize that Master requires transparency in order to make wise and informed decisions about slave?
- **Discipline**: What is the nature and extent of Master's control? How is discipline to be administered? Are there any restrictions on forms of discipline? For example, you may wish not to use any type of BDSM implement that is also used for scening. The issue is that implements used for scening carry positive associations and related positive emotions. If you start using the same implement for punishment, you will lose some/most/all of those special and positive associations with that implement. Similarly, if the slave was punished in a particular way in the past—particularly by parents—that form of punishment may now trigger land mines—you'll want to discuss that in the contract.
- **Finance:** Explain how pre-existing wealth, as well as income subsequent to the contract, is to be handled. For example, during the training contract, you may not wish to address any aspect of your slave's finances—just mark that section "reserved". On the other hand, if your slave candidate is very experienced (has lived as a slave for many years), he/she may expect to surrender personal control over their finances.
- **Duration:** How long is your contract? Under what conditions—and following what procedure—can it be terminated? (This is a hotly discussed topic. In the gay community, there is a tendency to spend some time getting to know one another before extending a contract without a termination date—a

There is no such thing as a cookie-cutter contract for this kind of relationship. You have to tailor this—or any other preexisting contract—to your own situation. These contracts are only included as examples, not as models.

contract for life. Among the heterosexual M/s movement, there is a much stronger tendency to create a series of staged contracts that carry termination dates. There is a substantial camp that believes that a contract must have a termination date in order to be realistic. There is another substantial camp who want their contracts to have termination dates because they recognize that the slave (and even the Master) may change a great deal during this experience, and Master wants to be able to reevaluate the slave every year or so, in light of their experiences together.)

Training or "getting to know you" contracts

Opening Statement: This contract represents our mutual understanding and agreement and Master and slave are mutually bound during this contracted period.

This is a voluntary contract between _____ and _____ dated: _____ that is intended to last from _____ to _____.

There is no assurance whatsoever that Master will extend a new contract to _____ at the end of this period.

Purpose: This contract has been prepared as a method of clarifying our mutual intent as we explore one another's interpersonal, social, and sexual wants and needs before moving on to a more expanded Master/slave contract.

This is a period when each of us is endeavoring to learn more about the other. Slave is seeking to determine whether the level of service and obedience that Master seeks from a slave matches what this slave can offer; Master is seeking to determine whether what this slave offers in terms of skills, knowledge, and heart meet Master's wants and needs. Both slave and Master are also exploring whether Master's leadership style and teaching style matches slave's following abilities and learning style.

During this period, we will each be assessing the other across key dimensions, including:

- Honesty
- Integrity
- Loyalty
- Trustworthiness

Since clear communication is based on open and honest communication, we both pledge ourselves to transparency: We each will answer questions put to us by the other as truthfully and completely as we are able. This obligation about truthfulness and honesty extends a bit further. Each of us are obliged to tell the other anything that we really know the other person **should** know. This includes topics/fears we really don't want to bring up for fear of upsetting the other person or because one of us didn't think to ask about it. *An error of omission is as deadly as an error of commission*.

Sex: In an effort to make this trial period as focused as possible, we each renounce sexual contact or play with others. During this contract period safer sex practices:

___ will be followed
___ will not be necessary

Markings and permanent piercings: During this period, Master will neither mark nor cause others to mark or introduce piercings other than those that the slave willingly wishes.

Correction and Punishment: Correction relates to protocol violations and includes Master expressing disappointment, minor *funishments* (swats), and more serious warnings against future reoccurrences of the unwanted behavior. During this initial phase, *punishment* is not an appropriate response to any behavior on slave's part, as Master does not yet own slave as property and does not yet have authority to punish this person.

Master and slave recognize that this period together can be compared with a "dating" stage in a vanilla relationship. It is a period where we are each exploring similarities and dissimilarities. During this time of learning, if either Master or slave upsets or offends the other, both parties agree to sit down and work through such upsets using talking stick protocols. (Note: *Talking sticks* were discussed earlier in the section on *Processing Mutual Hurts*.)

_____   _____
Master's signature   Date

_____   _____
slave's signature   Date

Long-term contracts
Contracts are so individualized that I don't want to take more time providing examples here. There are only two Websites that I'd send you to for contracts:
- *Negotiated Boundaries* contract for the enslavement term: *www.asubmissivesjourney.com/contract.html*
- Best contract I've ever seen—highly recommended: *http://everything2.com/title/a+real-life+slave+contract*

Collars

Okay: you know that collars are a visible symbol of your status. You know that they tell others that you are in a relationship with someone. You also know that collars don't say what kind of relationship you're in, just that you are in one. As people tend to fall into lust before they fall into logic, and as our community considers a collar to be a significant event, both of you may want to consider a few things.

For starters, what do you bring to the table? Do your skills/interests match those of your potential partner? What's in it for you? Can you list your wants and needs? Are you intending to fulfill your partner's dreams as much as they are intending to fulfill your? How will slave serve? How will Master *master*?

Many couples use the training period to determine their interpersonal *fit*. For such people the central key is: does this person have the raw potential to become my model Master or slave?

Here are some points to consider:
- Is the other person smart enough?
- Is the Master *worthy*? Is the slave *willing*? (This second phrase was developed some years ago by Master Steve Sampson and Master Skip Chasey)
- Can Master demonstrate ethical leadership? Will the slave say "yes" before the question is asked?
- Is the kind of service the slave offers the kind of service Master wants?
- Do you both agree to anything beyond a monogamous relationship? (For example, a polyamorous or swinging lifestyle on top of the M/s dynamic?)

Your conclusions guide your next steps.

Meaning of collars
Collars are usually—but not always—associated with contracts. As I said a few paragraphs ago, they are the visible symbol of a power exchange or authority transfer dynamic.

Collars have varying degrees of significance for people in the BDSM community. By wearing a collar, a person may wish to make it known that he or she is submissive. Wearing a collar may similarly be a signal to others that the submissive is owned by—or is in a relationship with—a Dominant. It may also be a tangible symbol of the relationship, itself. A lockable collar may further symbolize the transfer of power from the submissive to the Dominant who holds the key.

A person wearing a collar to symbolize their relationship with another is said to be **collared**. Some people conduct formal *collaring ceremonies* that are regarded as effectively solemnizing their relationship in the same way as a marriage ceremony.

As a fashion accessory, collars are becoming more common, but not sufficiently so that they would go unnoticed, particularly when worn by men. Many choose to wear their collars only when in private with their partners or with other members of the BDSM community. As BDSM practices move increasingly into middle class society, the role of the collar is also changing. Sometimes, couples who also practice 24/7 M/s and D/s relationships adopt collars that can pass as ordinary chokers or jewelry necklaces that can be worn discreetly in public.

Types of Collars

Unlike the Leather community, those in the not-Leather (BDSM) community often use different stages (or levels) of collaring. While individuals may assign various names to designate the significance of the collar to their partner, the general sequence goes like this:

The *collar of consideration* is the first stage and is roughly analogous to announcing that you're "going steady" with someone. This collar can be removed by the s-type at any time with no ill will, and the relationship would be ended. The community will take no particular notice if this level of collar does not transition into the next level.

Next comes the *training collar,* roughly analogous to an engagement ring; it indicates a deepening relationship in which the submissive is being prepared by the Master to serve to the standards that Master wishes. During this period the potential slave may ask to be released, but the break is considered to be more serious and painful for both parties. The community will realize that you tried to build a relationship and it didn't work out. Again, not a big deal: we're all searching.

Finally, the *full slave collar* is analogous to a wedding band, and at this point, the submissive is considered to be a formal slave, owned by the Master. In the Leather community, this stage is considered permanent. This bond would only be broken if the slave is released (or sought release) for some extraordinary reason. Simple failure of service is not adequate grounds for release, since that would show *control failure* on Master's part, as well as *performance failure* on the slave's part. As with engagement and wedding rings, there are traditions with collars in regard to materials and colors that are appropriate to each level, and they usually become more elaborate as the stages progress. At this level, Masters often conduct formal collaring ceremonies with close friends; the community-at-large now knows that you are an

M/s couple. A break-up at this level will send ripples through your community. As I discuss elsewhere in this book, experience has shown that those couples who perform "uncollaring" ceremonies upon the dissolution of their M/s relationship squelch rumors and gossip about the breakup.

Personally, I gave my former slave a *training collar* before I gave her a *collar of consideration*. My view was that I wanted to assess her ability to adjust both to me, personally, and to the lifestyle before I became too heavily invested. I also reversed the significance of the collars. That is, she was free to terminate the *training phase* of our relationship, but once she possessed the *collar of consideration*, it was like being engaged. Due to our particular situation, I extended that initial three-month training collar for two additional three-month periods. Hey: there are no *rules* here, just suggestions.

House collars (**collars of protection**) are sometimes used to indicate to others in clubs, homes, and in organizations that provide social spaces that the submissive is under the protection of your House and is to be approached with respect. I have seen protection collars used for submissives who are not yet ready to make their own choices and need time to learn.

We (Master and I) have extended protection collars to new submissives who wanted a buffer between over-enthusiastic Doms and their panties.

Protocols

Since I have already written a book on protocols (*Protocol Handbook for the Leather slave: Handbook of theory and practice*) I'm only going to make a few bullet points in this section.

Command-and-control is required for Person A to get what they want. If Person A only has *command*, then the result will be random, undefined. "Get me a hamburger" will result in a randomly prepared piece of ground beef. For Person A to get a hamburger prepared the way they wish it to be prepared, Person A must execute *control* over how the hamburger is prepared. Thus, M/s is based on command-and-

control, and control is expressed by Person A as a list of steps to follow to prepare hamburgers. These steps are referred to as *protocols*.

- Protocols are the written procedures for *doing things the way Master wishes them done*. You can think of it as Master's "User's Guide." You are coming together as adults in this new and unusual structure and slave wishes to know how to please Master. By writing down what pleases Master, slave has standards to work from. This avoids the uncomfortable situation wherein Master says to do X in Y fashion this week, then forgets the way he said he wanted it done and corrects slave the next time X comes up and tells her to do it in style Z.
- All skill-based activities (dancing, martial arts, construction) have learning curves. You can only move on to the more advanced material after having mastered the basics. It's the same thing in an M/s relationship. Until slave has mastered the art of serving Master as he or she wishes, slave is not ready to move on to the more interesting things that Master can offer.
- Protocols are a moment-by-moment recognition of the authority-imbalance in your relationship. At the same time, they remind you that you are **not** in a vanilla relationship. Used this way, protocols help to strengthen the bond between you. You can also create protocols that daily affirm how important each of you is to the other.
- slave's use of protocols triggers Master's sense of pride of ownership.
- By establishing protocols to handle stressful situations, you have added options to break old and habitual response patterns when you encounter upsets.
- Protocols are a daily affirmation of consent.
- Protocols can be viewed as *stage management*. You can use protocols to set the scene in your home that helps you to manage the relationship.
- You can't rely on wisdom, protocols, or rules that you've seen others use or that you've heard about or read about: you must build all of these entirely from within yourself for each slave you own. Protocols flow from who you are; they are an outward expression of what you value.

Chapter 6
Core Mechanics of M/s Relationships

Experience amply demonstrates that one's degree of competence in three (learnable) skills stand out above all else when it comes to the degree of success and fulfillment people express in their Master/slave relationships. These three areas are: leadership, communication, and training. This chapter is devoted to highlighting some of the key factors for each topic.

About leadership

People come in all makes and models. Big, little, short, and tall, yes? It's really the same when it comes to thinking about a person's leadership skills. Some people are strong leaders and other people really need to be kept away from leadership roles.

This section discusses some ways that personality issues can impact Master's leadership style.

Leadership as a concept

While you can't grow two inches as an adult, you can learn to change your own skills and behavior to move yourself around on the leadership scale (below) that contrasts leadership styles with respect to *commitment to people* and *commitment to tasks*. While most people fall somewhere near the center-point of this grid, here is how you'd be described if you tested out to be at the extreme points.

> **A-6:** excellent people skills, not committed to tasks
> **F-6:** excellent with tasks and also excellent with people-management skills
> **A-1:** primarily self-indulgent: doesn't focus on tasks and isn't good with people
> **F-1:** strongly task-oriented but lacks people skills

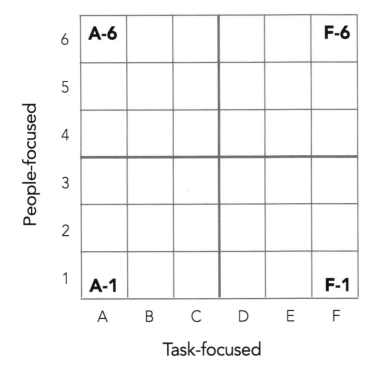

So: let's see how these characteristics (at the extremes) apply to leadership in the context of an M/s relationship.

F-1-type leaders (focused on tasks and not people) will appear to be *authoritarian*. They will be hard to live with. They won't much care whether or not slave wants to cooperate, they expect slave to do what they are told without question or debate. When things go wrong the

F-1-type leader will look for someone to blame rather than analyze the situation and accept some amount of personal responsibility. This is the Master who is never wrong even if he/she is totally wrong. Without people skills, this leader is intolerant of outside ideas or criticism; a slave to such a Master will find it hard to feel that they are contributing to the relationship and growing within it.

F-6-type leaders (good both at task-management and people skills) lead by example and encourage a team model designed to benefit themselves and those around them while simultaneously strengthening bonds among all under his/her direct control. There is an obvious and direct path between this conceptual model and the *team model* of M/s structure. In the business world, leaders such as these are well known for leading some of the most productive teams in Corporate America.

A-6-type leaders love their relationships with people and are afraid of jeopardizing them. They may use rewards to induce cooperation rather than risk relationship upsets by using either legitimate power or coercive power. In the M/s world, this would be the Master whose slave knows that he/she will never be reigned in, even for overt acts of resistance and boundary-testing. This is a Master whose attitude is: "Look, you know what I want you to do, so please get with the program and do it." The slave may run this relationship more than Master, for there are no consequences for bad behavior.

A-1-type people who have fallen into leadership positions are probably as miserable as they make those around them. Committed neither to accomplishing tasks nor maintaining interpersonal relationships, they tend to allow those working with them to do whatever they wish so long as they, themselves, are left alone. Those working around this type of person develop work-arounds and are usually embroiled in power struggles within their group. I've only known of a few cases where this description fit someone self-identifying as a Master. In both cases, the people realized that they couldn't carry out Master roles and withdrew from the relationship altogether.

This, then, raises the personal question about whether or not you have leadership power.

Leadership power

So: do *you* have leadership power? Some people seem to be born leaders; some people seem to be born followers. Corporations spend countless hours training their employees to assume leadership positions; the U.S. Military is almost wholly devoted to teaching leadership skills. In both cases, the climb becomes steeper as you near the top. The final ascent is tremendously intense and competitive. As your advancement depends more and more on the application of your learned skills, you'll notice that fewer and fewer of your old friends are there with you.

It's quite similar with Master/slave relationship structures. When you first found the world of BDSM you had lots of friends starting out with you—whether you were a D-type or an s-type. When you formed your first D/s relationship, many of your friends were doing the same. But, as your interest and learning shifted away from D/s and more towards M/s or O/p, you found that your old friends seldom kept up with you: They weren't interested in going to MAsT meetings; their interpersonal issues no longer paralleled your interpersonal issues.

Have you ever wondered about their choices versus your choices? Have you ever wondered why you and your D/s friends drifted apart? While I've never studied this particular schism, my gut feeling is this: The cutting line between D/s and M/s concerns *ownership*. Once Master owns a living person, Master's attention and focus shifts inward to the relationship. I suspect that the attention to personal leadership, communication, and training that comes with responsibility for another person (and that are not normally concerns of a D/s couple) causes you slowly to drift from your friends who remain in BDSM-based D/s structures because you have increasingly less in common. Just a guess.

At any rate, these new concerns over leadership now raise new and thoughtful questions. Can Master stand firm on an ethical or moral issue when the situation demands it? Can Master show empathy and compassion instead of wearing a mask? Does Master have a clear vision (that can be concisely articulated) for the Family's future? Do those who are following Master's lead doing so with enthusiasm, high energy, and conviction? If not, why not? Does Master need to learn more about motivational leadership?

It is for reasons such as these that I often tell people that structured relationships are among the most complex and sophisticated relationships that I know of. When they ask me why I believe this, I explain that unlike most relationships, these sorts of structures are concerned on a daily bases with topics such as *mindfulness, intent, purpose, honor, integrity, loyalty*, and *trust*. I explain that these are topics that come up almost daily for most M/s couples that I know.

So let me move in closer for some details of leadership. Let me start by asking Masters: How do you execute the responsibility of your command? You've been given authority over another person: how, exactly, do you do that ethically and responsibly? If your slave were giving you a performance evaluation, what would it say? Here's a list of traits of successful leaders (scrounged from multiple sources). How are you doing? For slaves: How's your Master doing? Might it be time to sit down and challenge yourselves to ask what you're doing with your one shot at life on Earth?

Successful leaders...
- Observe with application (they act on their observations).
- Take copious notes and record them in a way that you can go back and review them (memory is fallible).
- Know how to listen well; know how to distinguish between background chatter and important issues; know how to ask clear, courteous and incisive questions. (There are a number of outstanding books about *leading with questions*.)
- Welcome ideas. (The ideas of others help to shake you out of the ruts of your insular reality.)
- Value time highly. (You're going to run out of it sooner than you expected. It's not gong to be fun to figure this out when you reach age 70.)
- Set goals as a matter of routine.
- Try to understand a situation before commenting on it (successful leaders don't jump to conclusions.)
- Always anticipate achievement (successful leaders don't reinforce negative self-thoughts.)
- Know how to organize their approach to challenges
- Have a five-year plan for success.

- Realize that they, not others, ultimately control their own success.
- Brainstorm alternatives to tough decisions (use *consensus management techniques.* For more information do an Internet search for "consensus management").
- Celebrate achievements; shrug off setbacks.
- Develop and use a support network.
- Always stand for integrity.
- Remind them that every day is a new opportunity.
- Keep them in top physical condition.
- Always remain open to learning new ideas

Note: The above list is attributed variously to Whitt N. Schultz, H. Gordon Selfridge, or Bob Adams', *Streetwise Business Tips.* Adams Media Corp. I've made some additional notes on some of the lines.

Applying this last section to your M/s lifestyle, you might consider taking each of these bullet points and opening it up. Tease out the implications of each bullet for your personal situation. For example, take the bullet that reads: "Always anticipate achievement." What can this mean in your world? How well do you support your slave, emotionally? Are you always *catching him/her doing something right*? Do you bring home occasional treats/gifts of love? Do you know your slave's favorite things—and do you make sure their favorites make it into your life, too? I know, sounds like a marriage. It's far more than that, of course—spousal support is only the support base for a highly evolved *structured relationship*.

The fact that you own a slave does not excuse you from reinforcing in your slave extreme feelings of love and warmth toward you as Master and an appreciation for how lucky your slave is that you accepted him/her. Often, my slave would ask me what I want for the evening. My unswerving answer is: "What I want is that tomorrow morning you open your eyes in bed and you say to me: 'Wow! What a fabulous night we had last night, thank you so much.'"

Demonstrate leadership

Demonstrating leadership involves mental discipline. As much as anything else, it is a visible expression of your mindset. Since your mindset is based on your beliefs, the path to demonstrating leadership starts with having the ideas that enable you to develop a belief structure that you are a leader. Here are some suggestions along those lines.

The following list was provided by Master Kurt (Florida) and slave john and was included in their class handout some years ago. I consider these seven points extraordinarily important and recommend them to you without reservation.

- Affirm strong, ongoing commitment by both partners to the M/s lifestyle.
- Remain flexible in negotiating terms of the partnership.
- Integrate dominance (control) and submission (service) dynamics into everyday activities.
- Engage in ongoing sexual/BDSM activities that bond partners to one another while reinforcing their self-identities.
- Recognize that both partners must share common values and interests outside of the M/s lifestyle to maintain a long-term union.
- Maintain transparent communication between partners.
- Periodically reset/recalibrate the relationship to ensure that partners remain interested in and connected to one another.

I have found that in addition to traditional advice found in books on leadership, leaders writing about their personal beliefs express certain common viewpoints that I find interesting. I'm including some in this section. On a personal note, these are some of the key ideas that have for years influenced my relationships with my partners.

Watch your Thoughts…

Watch your thoughts, they become words.
Watch your words, they become actions.
Watch your actions, they become habits.
Watch your habits, they become character.
Watch your character, it becomes your destiny.
—Frank Outlaw

The importance of acting…

> To look is one thing.
> To see what you look at is another.
> To understand what you see is a third.
> To learn from what you understand is still something else.
> But to act on what you learn is all that really matters.
> —Taoist saying

Here are some other ideas that may demonstrate the kinds of thoughts that can help you evolve or hone your mental attitude about leadership.

- A commitment is doing what you said you would do long after the mood you said it in has passed. (Variously attributed)
- Be bold about ideas, tentative about people. (Anon.)
- You can never solve the problem using the same logic that created it in the first place. (Einstein)
- Vision without action is a daydream. Action without vision is a nightmare. (Japanese proverb)
- There is not a *right* way to do a *wrong* thing. **Knowing** what's right doesn't mean much unless you **do** what's right. (Theodore Roosevelt)
- The one important thing I have learned over the years is the difference between taking one's work seriously and taking one's self seriously. The first is imperative; the second is disastrous. (Margot Fonteyn)
- Tact is the art of making a point without making an enemy. (Isaac Newton)
- Professionals are people who can do their job when they don't feel like it. Amateurs are people who can't do their job when they DO feel like it. (Deepak Raj)
- If you have tried to do something and failed, you are vastly better off than if you had tried to do nothing and succeeded. (Richard Martin Stern)
- The average person has about 10,000 ideas per day; the problem is that same average person had 99.9% of those same ideas the day before. And the day before, and the day before. Actually, the hidden problem, here, is with overworked ideas. (Winston Churchill)

- Things don't change, we do; there is always a way if you're committed. (Anthony Robbins)
- In the long run, it's more orderly to convert chaos to system than to cover chaos with system. (Roger Zelazney)
- What you are afraid to do is a clear indicator of the next thing that you need to do. (Anthony Robbins)

Exuding personal power

Exuding (expressing) power is a shade different from demonstrating leadership. In the corporate world, those who are given leadership positions generally exude personal power.

In the most general way, power and authority either flows out from you or is ascribed to you. Some people, those who seem to be born leaders, exude authority and control even when taking a shower. Others, those not born with that particular attribute, may or may not learn it during their lifetime. Training in a few professions will teach leadership skills that include methods of projecting power (military or law enforcement), but most jobs and careers are most concerned about training people to be good team players, followers or workers.

You can also be given power by virtue of the position you hold in a company or in a community. Thus, you can find people who are actually indecisive or socially inept who have substantial rank and power. This is certainly true for people who have inherited great wealth, and it is also true for people who are appointed to high government positions because they have been politically useful to someone.

This applies to Master/slave structures in important ways. Master has been given absolute authority over a slave, but Master may or may not exude much personal power. Master may not be much of a communicator, leader, or planner. Master may have stumbled into this position of Master, yet the slave is looking to this person for inspired leadership.

You can easily see the potential for letdown.

As Master Jim Glass (Co-producer of *South Plains Leatherfest*) points out, successful Master/slave relationships thrive on a simple equation:

control plus *power* produces *respect*. As I've commented previously, a slave is not a boyfriend or girlfriend. This is not a vanilla relationship. A successful Master must master both the verbal and non-verbal techniques of exuding personal power.

But, how do you exude *personal power* if it does not come naturally to you? Where does *the control* come from? An Internet search may be helpful, but here are some bulleted notes. You should be able to take some of these ideas and do Internet and Amazon searches to get more material.

Ideas about developing *command presence*:
- Give a good first impression—every day. You don't want to look like an unmade bed.
  - Make a point of dressing well. Always wear clean, pressed clothing; dress professionally.
  - Others will judge you by the cleanliness of your car. Keep it clean, inside and out.
  - If you work in an office, keep it extremely clean and tidy.
- Be conscious of your physical stance.
  - Legs apart, shoulder width.
  - Hands to sides, NOT in front or in back.
  - Be careful to be *planted* and not to rock or sway.
  - Don't *lean* on anything.
  - How do you handle *down time*, time where you don't have something to do? Do you look bored and inattentive?
- Attend to how you *walk*. How you carry yourself portrays command presence or lack of it. Confidence is projected through your body language and how you verbally deal with individuals and groups.
  - Walk with intent. Don't shuffle your feet or use a sloppy walking style. Your walk should indicate your intent; communicate that you know where you are going and that you have a purpose in going there.
  - Walk with your head up, eyes alert, and be in control of your facial expression. You do not want to appear weak or vulnerable. You want to project the image

of someone who knows why they are where they are and who knows what they are doing. Consider taking martial arts training—it will teach you how to project power

o   Portray the image that you are in charge of the situation. The key is to be *outwardly confident*—even if on the inside you are scared out of your wits. You want your body language to convey confidence. (My personally favorite book on body language is: *What Every BODY is Saying: An Ex-FBI Agent's Guide to Speed-Reading People* by Marvin Karlins)

- Attend to how you *speak*.
  o   Your speech is not only a social class and economic status marker, it is another aspect of command presence. *More people than you think hear you speak.*
  o   Don't say too much—when you're silent, people take it to mean you're wise and thoughtful.
  o   Don't say anything that you don't have to say— *knowledge is power*: don't give it away.
  o   If you make a mistake, apologize and clean up your own mess. You are responsible for ensuring that your message is heard the way you intended it to be heard.
  o   Use a strong, well-modulated voice (practice being forceful with yourself in a mirror—preferably naked). (I knew a female police lieutenant who said she taught herself voice control by forcefully instructing a chair to remain just where it was. She went on to be an instructor in *command presence* at a police academy for a major East Coast city.)

- Observe yourself during a stressful situation. What would others see or hear from you when you're under stress?
  o   How do you visibly change what you were doing? What reactions do you display physically—including your facial expression?
  o   What do you say about the situation? Did you immediately *come present* and shift into *action mode*?
  o   Do you interpret the situation negatively or positively? Do you use the uncomfortable situation as an

> opportunity for positive change or dismiss it as a negative episode? Do you look outwardly to find someone responsible for the stressful situation you're in or start responding from your own ethical core to help to de-stress the situation? Are you *at the cause* of your personal reaction to the stress or *at the effect* of the situation?
> o Monitor yourself; practice being assertive without being domineering. Keeping your cool is also a big part of this.

Command presence boils down to how you present yourself in the world. When you enter a room do people come over to you just to be seen with you? Do you demonstrate that you're the kind of person who solves problems? Do you carry yourself with confidence? Do you ACT the part? Do you speak the part? If you can, then you have succeeded in developing command presence, which will enable you to flow naturally into the role of Master.

For those of us who do *not* yet have these characteristics, this list may help you to understand the often-heard expression that, "You have to master yourself before you can Master another." Again, that is why—in my personal experience—successful Masters in M/s relationships tend to be over 35 (or be particularly gifted at interpersonal and social skills).

About Communication

In my experience, communication breakdowns result from a collection of evils. The communications mess usually starts when the speaker is speaking only from their own viewpoint and hasn't factored in the other person's viewpoint. As a result, the speaker sends out messages that are phrased in the speaker's (rather than the listener's) language. Among other things, that means that the speaker has made assumptions about how much the listener knows or remembers about the topic being discussed: also, the speaker is likely to be speaking partly in a private shorthand or code.

Along these lines, communication hick-ups often occur when the speaker uses imprecise words, forcing the listener to interpret the speaker's meaning ("You know, like when they sort-of fudge some of the words to avoid being, like, too direct, right?") As if this isn't enough, a range of other distractions further contaminates the overall communication process. For example, even while speaking and listening, both people are simultaneously making judgments about each other, about the environment around them, and about what they're going to have for dinner. This keeps them from being fully present with one another. Bottom line: each party remembers most verbal exchanges very differently. While each party thinks they understood the communication, if you administered an objective test, their respective understandings would be revealed to be substantially different.

I'm not going to start down the path of teaching communication skills in a book on M/s relations. For now, I'll just make some observations. I've tried to summarize some key points in a variety of important areas.

These areas are interrelated: how clearly you speak your message ties in to two *listening* concepts: first, how well your reply matched what was said (how well *you* were listening) as well as how well you are able to tailor your reply to the characteristics of the person with whom you're speaking. From there, I'll touch on *transference and projection* before ending up with *upsets*.

Speaking

I distinguish between *talking* and *speaking*. One *talks to* someone or *speaks with* someone. In my view, talking is one-way—it's lecturing. By its very nature, lecturing reinforces a knowledge and/or power imbalance and puts the listener in a one-down position. This distinction is very important both in training (where you may wish to sound as though you know something) and in emotionally loaded discussions (where you're likely to get into trouble).

The reason you can get into trouble *talking to* your partner during an emotionally charged exchange is that when you sound "authoritative" you also sound *parental*. Those who know about the communications field called Transactional Analysis (TA) realize that speaking in parent voice can trigger (or sustain) your listener responding in child voice (filled with words communicating emotion). Once you know a bit about TA, you'll learn how to extract yourself from this kind of very upsetting loop by moving into what is called *adult* voice.

All of which is to say that the path to emotionally calm conversations involves *speaking with* someone. Let's tease this apart for a minute. All communication involves the following mix:

- Someone wishes to communicate a message;
- They say something that may or may not communicate that message clearly;
- Even if the person speaking was actually successful in speaking the words that carried their intended message, the person receiving the message does so within the context of social, political, and economic filters that have been created from their lifetime of experiences (most strongly influenced by their childhood experiences around which they built life-rules that kept them from emotional or physical pain);
- In an effort to make what was said fit into their universe, the listener interpreted what they *thought* they heard and make it mean something.

The something that they make it mean may not be precisely what the person meant to communicate.

Speaking is rather like sex: we think we do it well because we've been doing it our entire lives. We seldom sit down to study the topic. Unfortunately, the consequences translate equally to mediocre sex and imprecise communication. You might reflect for a minute…

- What evidence do you have that you are able to communicate clearly, confidently, and persuasively? (In your work life, are you looked upon as a particularly clear communicator?)
- Do your ideas have *selling power*? Do other people generally follow your ideas?
- Have you read books or taken courses in effective communication strategies?
- When you speak, do you use simple words, short sentences, and clear word-pictures?
- When your partner describes an experience or a concern, do you take the time to listen actively and to respond in a

way that makes the other person feel acknowledged and respected? Does the person with whom you are speaking feel valued and validated?

Just before we move on to the section on *listening*, there is a transition stage: it's called **active listening** and it is the bridge between speaking and listening for both parties. While I really would like you to look it up on the Internet, in brief active listening involves this: When Person A says something, Person B restates what Person A said and gets Person A to agree that Person B actually understood what they had said. Only at that point does Person B speak a reply to the initial statement. This form of speaking provides three immediate benefits:

- It improves the quality of the conversation, as it slows down the conversation to give each person a time to think.
- It eliminates most areas of misunderstanding that result from a person making a response to some aspect of a statement that they have either misheard or misinterpreted.
- It takes much of the emotional loading out of a conversation enabling all parties to remain calm.

Listening

I suppose that one of the most common issues that arise between couples (whether or not involved in an M/s structure) is that one or the other feels that they're not being heard. Perhaps it's not too surprising, but like other skills, this one can be improved through practice. In my experience, even realizing that there are different listening levels has helped me to focus and be mindful when listening to others. I pass these on to you in the hopes you find them equally useful.

For starters, *listening* begins with basic sound discrimination when you are first born and winds its way through various stages to end up either as your friend or enemy once you hit *deep communication*.

Listening takes many forms, but this list of eight of the most common categories are all we need to give you a good understanding of the topic.

Discriminative listening is the most basic type of listening, for it requires you to assign meaning to sounds. This is where you learn how to

"The way we communicate with others and with ourselves ultimately determines the quality of our lives."

—Anthony Robbins

interpret voice inflections and emotional nuances. During a conversation, the richness of your understanding depends upon your skills at recognizing and interpreting the speaker's emotional cues.

Discriminative listening is closely allied to *discriminative observation*: observing muscular and skeletal movements that signify different meanings. (In this area, I highly recommend the book: *What Every BODY is Saying: An Ex-FBI Agent's Guide to Speed-Reading People* by Joe Navarro and Marvin Karlins)

Comprehension listening means that you have the capacity to understand what was said. At the simplest level, it's an issue of vocabulary combined with language skills. The fact that you're reading this book means that you've already mastered comprehension reading, so—presumably—you also know how to understand when someone speaks to you. But, here's the trouble: comprehension listening breaks down quickly in three common situations:
- The speaker uses imprecise words.
- The speaker uses filler words.
- The speaker is using coded or indirect speech.

Using imprecise words: I call these "mush" words. They are words that mean different things to different people. "That was a lovely dinner, thank you." can mean that you liked the way the food was prepared or it can mean that you liked the ambiance of the entire evening. Since this is social etiquette, you're not likely to spend a lot of time asking the speaker to clarify what they meant by "lovely dinner." Now, take the sentence, "You're an honorable person." In the first place, tonal inflection can generate quite different meanings. In the second place, without a lot more discussion, there is no way of knowing wither the speaker's and the listener's meaning of *honorable* is close to the same.

Using filler words in sentences requires you, as the listener, to guess what the speaker is trying to say. People use filler words when they don't know a subject well and hope that a filler word will disguise this reality. Take this sentence: "Like, it's like hard, you know, to get much action when you're not really in your groove, man; you know what I mean, right?"

> "The difference between the right word and the almost right word is the difference between lightning and a lightning bug."
>
> —Mark Twain

- Is the speaker saying that he doesn't get laid much because he doesn't have his act together?
- Is the speaker a bookie saying that he's having trouble getting people to bet with him because he's had a string of losses?
- Is the speaker playing a pinball machine and complaining that he keeps losing games because he's in a losing streak?

Who knows? Sure, these are extreme cases, but in structured relationships where communication clarity is supposed to be so important, lucidity and eloquence count. Oh, and short pithy sentences also help; they're easier to follow.

Using coded or indirect speech. "Whenever we had another man over for sex play, my husband would always have to clean up." Clean up? As in, the visitor didn't help to clean up before leaving? How rude; I bet he didn't get invited back. "No," she said. "That's not what that means: when our guest would leave I'd not have been sexually satisfied and so my husband would have to fuck me until I came." Oh. Got it.

We all speak in some variety of shorthand, but when it comes to sensitive topics—sex, arguing, emotional upset—imprecise words sidetrack the conversation as the listener appears to the speaker to be jumping from topic A to topic B when, in fact, the speaker's word choice is leading the listener to reply in ways that the speaker thinks are off-topic. The speaker is getting angry that they're not being heard; the listener is getting traumatized that they don't quite seem to understand what the speaker is saying.

The two of you are going to have to work this one on our own simply to be able to understand one another.

Critical listening enables you to evaluate and judge what is said—presuming that the speaker is using clear and direct speech. Critical listening requires that you assess the *content* of a message and also relate that content to your own knowledge of that topic even as you must simultaneously interpret what is said in the context of cultural/societal rules. Critical thinking works best if you develop some helping tactics. It will help if you learn not to become distracted by self-talk (for example, if the speaker misuses a word or says something that you believe is not true) or by splitting your attention between the speaker's superficial message and also the speaker's subtext. (Subtext: some people don't clearly say what they mean, they use a kind of code or subtext to get around personally or socially uncomfortable topics. As a listener, you risk becoming distracted as you try to decipher the sub-text while simultaneously staying present with the ongoing conversation. That's a heavy task: some are much better at it than others.)

Biased listening can occur for a number of reasons. Perhaps the most common is that the speaker says something that triggers you. You react by becoming defensive, angry, or sad. When that happens, your brain shifts its focus away from the speaker and causes you to focus on yourself. When this occurs, you'll only hear part of the message. At this stage, you may further misinterpret what is being said based on your own stereotypes, insecurities, and assumptions about the speaker and/or the topic being discussed. It is *very common* for a speaker to say "X" and for the listener to hear something wildly different—and then act on what they *thought* they heard. In an M/s structure, Master is responsible for recognizing when this has happened and to go back and track down the root of the misunderstanding. It's important to take that step if you expect to prevent the same type of misinterpretation in the future.

Appreciative listening occurs when you're in a good mood and listening to something you enjoy. This could be music, poetry or maybe even the melodious tone of your Master or slave's voice.

Sympathetic listening is used when we care about the other person and show this concern in the way we pay close attention and express our sorrow for their ills and happiness at their joys. (By the way, *empathetic listening* requires us to go beyond sympathy to seek a truer understand about how others are feeling. This requires excellent discrimination and close attention to the nuances of emotional signals. When we are being truly empathetic, we actually feel what the speaker is feeling.)

Relationship listening is most common when the relationship is new and each verbal interaction is adding to your pool of knowledge about the other person. This form of listening also occurs when there is an upset and you are trying to understand the other person's point of view.

Therapeutic listening contains risks if you're not trained in its use. With some trepidation I'm going to include it here. Psychologists and trained counselors use *therapeutic listening* to help clients understand, change, or develop in some way. That is, a client brings a problem to the counselor who listens with a "therapeutic ear" and replies in very specific ways that encourage the client to explore their issue.

Now, let's bring this setting to an M/s household after work one day. Master notices that slave is upset. Master begins to ask slave about their day. slave has had something happen and wants to *vent* about it. Master, not recognizing that slave is "venting," decides to be Helpful. Right now, every woman reading this book is giggling. But the men are lost, so I'll keep going.

Often, women wish to relate an experience just to get it out of their systems. The very *last* thing that they want is someone to tell them what they *should have done* or what they *should do tomorrow to fix it*. If you're not trained in listening for word prompts that signal emotional states, you risk replying in *parent voice* (making parental-like pronouncements and offering solutions) rather than reply in *adult voice* (that is neutral and free of emotions). Replying with *coulds* and *shoulds* (in an authoritative, parent voice) will likely trigger a negative emotional reaction from the listener. That's the polite way of saying that you'll make matters much worse and probably causes your slave to drop into *child voice* (filled with emotional statements). My advice: beware, for you're about to have an emotional meltdown. If you're curious about ways that word choice can help or hurt your more serious relationship discussions, you can look up *Transactional Analysis*.

Improper listening is as damaging as improper speaking. They are equal sides of the communications equation. So: what can you do? You can become a better listener.

How can you practice *good listening habits*? Here are some suggestions:

Give full attention: The first habit of listening is to pay attention to the person who is speaking. Give them your full attention—and visibly so. Attend not only with your ears but with your whole body. Turn to face them. Gaze intently at them. The trick to *full attention* is to do it from inside your head, not just by moving your body. If you can be truly interested (which is often just a matter of attitude) then your body will happily follow your mind.

Help them to speak: Sometimes the speaker is having difficulty getting their point across. Maybe they are not that good at speaking or are seeking to explain a complex concept. You can help them and yourself by positive encouragement. One good approach is to ask positive questions, both to test your own understanding and also to demonstrate interest.

Support the person: Show your consideration of the other person through your actions. Help the person to feel good about themselves. Remember: the person listening to you has a different value set and has had a world of different life-experiences: they may bring a different (and useful) perspective to the discussion—and they may know things about what you are saying that you don't know. If you find that you're disagreeing with what you're hearing, it's prudent to disagree with what is being said rather than with the *person*. Show your acceptance of their right to differ with you while stating your opposition to what they say.

These brief discussions of speaking and listening skills plays into this next section about transference and projection.

Transference and projection

Speaking and listening are tremendously affected by transference and projection. Speaking personally, I think that these issues have given me more trouble over the years than any other aspect of communication.

In psychology, *transference* refers to the unconscious process of redirecting feelings about one person to another person. For instance, you might mistrust somebody who shares some of an ex-partner's manners, voice, or physical looks. Or, you may feel submissive to someone who resembles one of your parents or someone you have viewed as an authority figure.

Psychological *projection* (or projection bias) is the term used to describe an ego defense mechanism wherein you attribute (or *project*) your own unacceptable or unwanted thoughts or/and emotions to another person. This occurs because you're sensitive to (dislike) some aspect of your own behavior and when you see someone else exhibiting somewhat similar behavior, you may react negatively to that person even though this other person hasn't yet done anything to demonstrate unworthiness or distrust.)

For example, projection occurs when Person A projects his/her own interpretation of an act onto Person B and then reacts to Person B *as if* they had reacted as Person A imagined that they did. This situation can occur when one person is not listening carefully to another, when one person is guilty about something and is trying to shift the blame, or when a person projects personal insecurities or weaknesses onto the *other partner and then reacts to those projections*.

Worse, the person being blamed is not at fault. Either there has been some serious breach of trust perceived by the person doing the blaming or the person doing the blaming is personally insecure about something and is lashing out.

- If the projection concerns a perceived breach of trust of your partner, you probably have a communications challenge.

- If the projection is not specific and occurs rather randomly, it may well result from low self-esteem. In that case, the one doing the projecting is likely to have a lot of personal work to do.

It doesn't take a rocket scientist to realize that once one person starts reacting to their own projected insecurities, the relationship has headed down a path filled with misunderstandings, hurt feelings, and mutual bitterness.

If one partner's projections go unchecked, both partners will increasingly grow wary of one another. One partner is seeing dragons under the bed while the other partner can't figure out what they did to trigger this negative pattern.

Which now brings us to *upsets* to round out this part of the book

Upsets

Years ago and far away (I think it was during my *est* training in 1975) I first learned about upsets. What I learned forever changed my way of thinking about them.

From *est* (*Erhard Seminars Training*, now *Landmark Education Forum*) I learned that to say, *I am upset* sends a message to your brain (and to those around you) that your *state of being* is upset, not fully in control, toppled. Once you declare yourself to be in an upset state of mind, others respond to you as an upset person.

"The most important thing in communication is hearing what isn't said."

—Peter Drucker

Since people have their own learned patterns of dealing with upset people, you can easily find people giving you wildly differing opinions about what you should do about your upset. Often, all this conflicting "good advice" serves to keep you stirred up inside: the reactions of others keep you upset. This is not good. Nobody knows the *real you*; they have no way of understanding enough about the filters you've established since infancy to know how to help you calm down.

The thing of it is, your own analysis of your own upset is based on your own self-knowledge. Translation: unless you've studied and practiced ways of controlling your emotional state, you're not a fit judge of your own emotional condition and you're not very likely to be able to control it.

In a practical sense, you're now *at the effect* of being upset; the person you become when you become upset is in charge of you. Your rational self has left the room in disgust. Still worse, the person at whom you direct your upset/anger could use that opportunity to manipulate you, as you're not fully in control of yourself, your upset is in control of you. Not a good position to be in if you think you're leading much more than a murder of crows.

You can teach yourself to interrupt your normal upset pattern.

When you sense you are getting upset, change your physical/emotional state. Stand up. Sit down. Stretch. Take three deep breaths. Go get a drink of water. Change your physical position as a way of buying time to get control over your emotional state. If you can stop the process of becoming upset and get control of yourself, you can then learn to **choose** your reaction. This isn't an overnight fix, but it suggests a path for gaining better self-control.

To help you choose your reaction, think about how you can be the cause of your reaction, rather than being at the effect of your reaction. Translation: Choose to h*ave an upset* rather than *being upset*. That's something like choosing to have an ice cream cone. In the same way that you can choose to have a chocolate or vanilla ice cream cone, you can learn to choose whether you will or will NOT have an upset. (Hint: You're likely to find that just before you're about to explode, you will sense some physical sensations. In my own case, the back of my scalp starts to tingle, providing me a second or two to act to change my response away from old an ineffective patterns of upset.)

You are going to have to make up your own method of breaking the action-reaction cycle to turn it into an action-action cycle. Ultimately, you are responsible both for your actions and reactions; actually, they're the same thing, but it may take you some time to realize that.

(Material like this comes from the world of Neuro-Lingusitic Programming—NLP. I strongly urge people to explore NLP and consider going through a training course. It's a game-changer. Your work life and personal life will both be improved as you learn more about sophisticated communication techniques.)

About Training

Purpose of training

Before you even start training, you might ask yourself: "What's the purpose of the proposed training?" At the most basic level, are you trying to train a slave for service or for submission? BIG difference.

"It takes all kinds to make a horse race," goes the old saying. In M/s relationships, that can mean that you and your partner may not learn the same way and that what motivates one of you does not motivate the other. Here are some topics to consider:

- What type of slave do you seek? (Personal Assistant? Major Domo? Companion? Sex slave?....)
- How can you train the slave for best effect? (There is no "one size fits all" type of training: you have to evaluate your partner's interests, learning capabilities, skills, etc, etc, even before you start the "training")
    - Will you use behavior modification or didactic learning or open learning?
- Is this a new slave or an experienced slave in relationship to type of and extent of training you're considering? (Clearly, a never-married female slave of 24 is a vastly different proposition than a mid-50s professional woman who has umpteen years of marriage behind her)
- What will you do if the slave does not appear to understand what you want? (Will you begin to read/study communication skills? You're going to have to tease apart whether the difficulty is with your way of speaking or with your slave's capacity to understand and apply your lessons.)
- What's motivating your slave to serve you? (Transactional service, devotional service, positional service? These are "slave motivations" and to learn more about them, I'd send you to

their source: Joshua Tenpenny and Raven Kaldera's book *Real Service*.)

- How current are you on *training theory*? (How much do you know about the different ways there are to reach people with various learning styles? Note: there's an important difference between teaching and training. Teaching concerns communicating a skill: training concerns communicating the application of a skill.)
  - Formal slave training, rather like Military boot camp, begins by severely limiting slave's rights: slave must earn rights and freedoms
  - More emotionally supportive training, for a slave who might be devastated by more firm handling and strict rules, may be rooted in *empathy*.
- How will your proposed training concurrently meet your slave's needs?
  - What if the slave rebels against the type of training that Master is providing? What if the slave has its own ideas about training and service?
  - "How can I serve him *my* way?"—"*If Master does not want it, it's not service*" notes Joshua Tenpenny and Raven Kaldera in their outstanding book *Real Service*.

Learning modalities

As I said in an earlier section, people take in and *process* information differently. That means that they learn differently. It's very important to understand these differences if you think that you're going to impart information to someone else.

Succinctly, people process information according to some combination of the five senses: sound, sight, touch, smell, and taste.

Aural learner: An aural learner (or auditory learner) tends to retain information more thoroughly when the information is reinforced through sound. Aural learning methods could include anything from musical notes to voice recordings or chants. For training purposes, you may have to speak to them rather than give them written instructions— or at least reinforce the written protocols with a thorough oral briefing.

If a person is high enough on the auditory scale, they may turn their *ear* towards you when you're speaking—rather than *look* at you.

In general, those who learn aurally:
- Like to read out loud.
- Are not afraid to speak up.
- Likes to provide oral (rather than written) reports.
- Is good at explaining things.
- Remembers names.
- Notices sound effects in movies.
- Enjoys music.
- Is good at grammar and foreign language.
- Reads slowly.

Within the relationship, aural learners may:
- Want to hear that you love them.
- Want you to **tell** them you love them.
- Want you to **tell them** what's right or wrong or what to do.

Auditory learners are likely to find it easy to derive the underlying meaning that someone is speaking by keying in on tonal changes and voice inflection. When memorizing, many auditory learners repeat the material out loud in order to remember how it sounded.

If you hear these phrases, the person processes auditorally:
- "I hear what you're saying."
- "That sounds right."
- "Have I told you…"

For training purposes, you should know that auditory (aural) processors:
- Follow spoken directions well.
- Can't keep quiet for long periods.
- Enjoy acting, being on stage.
- Can memorize material easily.
- Are good in study groups.

Auditory Learners Can Benefit from:
- Using word association to remember facts and lines.

- Recording (and later listening again to) long or complex directions/instructions.
- Watching videos.
- Repeating facts with eyes closed.
- Participating with others for group discussions.
- Using audiotapes for language practice.
- Typing notes after writing them.

Auditory learners are best at writing responses to lectures they've heard and at taking oral exams. They will have most trouble reading passages and writing answers about them in a timed test.

Visual learner: Visual learners tend to use images, pictures, color and other visual media to help them to learn. They incorporate imagery into their visualizations. They are likely to use highlighters when reading in order to make sure that the new material stands out from the rest of the text.

In general, visual learners:
- Are good at spelling but forget names;
- Need quiet study time;
- Have to think awhile before understanding something new;
- Like colors and fashion;
- Dream in color
- Understand/like charts;
- Are good with sign language;
- Cover the walls of their homes and offices with artwork or pictures;
- Wear clothes that are a little dressier than the average person; and
- Their homes may be a bit more tidy than average (not necessarily *clean*, but tidy).

Within the relationship, visual learners may communicate love by:
- Dressing nicely;
- Keeping the house tidy; and
- Decorating—including decorating the dining table, dinner plates, and walls.

If you hear phrases such as these, the person probably processes information through visual channels.

- Let's look at it differently.
- See how this works for you.
- I can't quite picture it.
- Let's draw a diagram or map.
- I'd like to get a different perspective.
- I never forget a face.
- I see what you're saying

This is a list of strategies that may help when training someone who learns visually.

- Use color, layout, and spatial organization in your associations, and use as many visual words in your communications as you can. Examples include: see, picture, perspective, imagine, visualize, and map.
- Use mind maps. Use color and pictures in place of text, wherever possible. If your lesson is not computer-based, make sure you have pens/markers of at least four different colors.
- Systems diagrams can help the person visualize the links between system elements. For example it might be helpful to color-code protocols of different priorities or protocols used at different times. Replace words with pictures, and use color to highlight major and minor links.
- The visual story technique can help someone memorize content that isn't easy to see.
- If you know anything about NLP (or Tony Robins' teachings) the *swish* technique for changing behaviors also works well for visual learners, as it relies on visualization.

Kinesthetic learner: Kinesthetic learners use their body and sense of touch to learn about the world. They frequently like sports and exercise and other physical activities such as gardening or woodworking. You like to feel things: you like to use exercise time to think through issues, ideas, and problems. You would rather go for a run or walk than sit at home if something is bothering you.

In general, those who learn kinesthetically:

- Use large hand gestures and other body language to communicate;
- Enjoy activities with physical touch—such as dancing; and
- Tend either to love the physical action of theme park rides or find that they upset their inner body sense too much and avoid them altogether.

If you hear phrases such as these, the person probably processes information through channels involving feeling and touching.

- That feels right to me.
- I can't get a grip on this.
- Stay in touch or get in touch with…
- That doesn't sit well with me.
- I have good feelings about this.
- My gut is telling me…
- I follow your drift.

For training purposes, here is some material to help you teach someone who processes information kinesthetically.

- Be physical. Focus on the physical sensations of what it is you are teaching. For example, if you're teaching a service protocol, have them focus on how they will feel as they are carrying out the service, the love it brings to them to serve correctly, etc.
- Describe the physical feelings of your actions. For example, a protocol for introducing your slave at a formal Leather event might sound something like this: "You feel calm and centered as you adjust your stance slightly behind my right shoulder for the *on point* position. You feel the thrill of excitement as I am beginning to introduce myself to Master X. You carefully note that your eyes are slightly down…"
- Use physical objects as much as possible. Have the kinesthetic learner physically touch objects as they learn about what they do. Flashcards can help them memorize information because they can touch and move them around.
- As writing and drawing diagrams are physical activities, don't neglect these techniques. Consider using an easel and pad and large color markers for your diagrams: you'll get more action from the drawing.

- Use breathing and relaxation to focus their state while they learn and perform. Focus the kinesthetic on staying calm, centered, relaxed, and aware. If you want to gain more control over their physical state, look up some references on autogenics (a technique used in sports training).
- Use role-play to practice skills and behaviors. Find ways to have the kinesthetic learner act out or simulate what you are teaching.

Within your relationship…
- Does your partner touch you?
- Does your partner specifically **not** touch you?
- **How** and **where** you touch your partner becomes another indication of how each of you prefer to take in information.

Think for a minute… if one of you is strongly kinesthetic and one of you is strongly something else, you guys might wish to spend some time discussing this difference.

I had a friend some years ago who was high-visual and his wife was high-kinesthetic. He needed intense focused time for his work. One day she came up behind him while he was deep in concentration and touched his shoulder in a gesture of love. He exploded in anger. By the way, that episode drove him to research teaching and learning styles and to then go through Neuro-linguistic Programming training (NLP).

Gustatory learner: Love to cook? Have a certain food you like just before sex or play? For some people, the *love* message translates into wanting to prepare complicated and sophisticated meals. If you're in a relationship where one of the partners enjoys cooking or enjoys dining experiences, you'll want to recognize that each meal as an *I love you* event and respond in kind.

For training purposes, it may be possible to link certain protocols to certain food rewards.

Olfactory learner: One (or both) of you may care a great deal about how the other person smells. In the first place, if your partner processes by smell, the greatest tip-off is that they sniffed your neck early in your relationship. You evidently passed that test, but now your cologne selection---and the smell of your home---become issues. As does her selection of perfumes.

For training purposes, it may be possible to link certain protocols to smells.

Teaching styles

If you're Master, you're a teacher. You're a teacher whether or not you've ever taught a class: it comes with the territory. Your success as Master depends substantially on your ability to teach/train your slave.

For starters, *teaching*—like most things in life—flows from your background, experience, values, and integrity. Thus, no two teachers are alike, and Masters must develop a personal teaching style that accounts for the slave's learning abilities. Unless you've been trained as a teacher, *that* can be a challenge. The best I can do, here, is to give you a thumbnail overview of five common teaching styles. You must select a little of this and a little of that, depending on how your slave responds to your instructions. For those of you who are professional educators, this will be a big yawn. For those of you who have never lead a workshop, taught a class, or facilitated a group discussion, this is meant to suggest some area for further study.

Authority Figure: The authority figure (Master) is the center of attention. slave is to focus on Master's direct instruction. In order to maintain control, any type of misbehavior must be dealt with quickly. Master maintains power through negative punishments that is swift and severe. This style of teaching is most common with recalcitrant students: while it may produce short-term gains, it is sure to build resentment and anger in a slave who seeks to serve Master and is doing its best to do so. Also, unless Master's training as a teacher is significantly greater than slave's training, slave may sense that Master is making shit up. That's not going to strengthen Master's authority/ wisdom in slave's eyes.

Authority Model: While the style of instruction is similar to that of the authority figure, in this case Master models the expected behavior. There is often a clear-cut discipline structure that is well understood by the slave. Day-by-day, Master builds confidence in slave's abilities and day-by-day, slave develops trust for Master.

Student-Centric: A student-centric teaching style focuses heavily on slave's specific learning styles and mental capacity. The lessons Master wishes slave to learn must accommodate slave's capabilities.

Facilitator: In this model, Master provides slave with an outline of what is to be learned/accomplished, access to the tools and materials to succeed, and then steps back to serve as a facilitator, as needed. Master does not meddle or hint. Facilitators trust that their student(s)/slave(s) will learn to be creative and derive answers mostly on their own. At the end of a significant activity, Master will discuss the outcome with slave.

(Note: one of the hardest things in life is to stand by and say nothing as you watch someone you care for fail at some task. However, as Charles F. Kettering said: "Learn how to fail intelligently, for failing is one of the greatest arts in the world.")

Delegator: This type of teaching style is known as the *hands-off* method. The delegator is very similar to the facilitator, but much more emphasis is placed on student-driven learning. Master would prepare a complex situations or problem that slave must resolve on their own or with the help of others that they must identify. Master allows slave to design and implement their own assessments and projects and reinforces the friendships and relationships amongst the slave's helping network. Master acts as a consultant, providing guidance and support only in times of great need.

No one teaching style will work in every situation. Remember, even though you may prefer one teaching style over another, you must find the style that works best for you and your slave(s). Try different styles to meet different objectives, and always challenge yourself to find ways to reach a successful outcome with your slave.

An aside: sometimes you'll find that regardless of how you try to train slave to do something, none of your strategies work. You may want your slave to perform in some fashion (or to learn something) that is simply outside their abilities. You're butting your head against a wall. You might as well tell them to grow two inches. In the words of the Kenny Rogers song, *The Gambler*, "You've got to know when to hold 'em, know when to fold 'em, know when to walk away, and know when to run."

Problem-solving approaches

I used to work for the U.S. Department of Justice's Law Enforcement Assistance Administration. We had a joke in our division that ran like this: *If your problem is that you don't think you have a problem, then you have a problem.*

In interpersonal relationships, one party often fails to see a problem that is crystal clear to any outsider. So, I'm going to take some time to discuss ways to identify and solve problems. First, let's start with how you even identify a problem.

In a broad way, there are two kinds of problems: skills problems and knowledge problems. I will tackle solutions/approaches to each kind of problem.

The material in the first part of this section is really, really helpful—as long as the problem you're about to tackle has to do with a desire to move the Family dynamic from one set of conditions to another set of conditions.

Frame the issues: Understand/explicate the problem. Often the *real* problem is to be able to describe the *core issue(s)* that are begging for solutions.

For example, it may help you to distinguish whether you have a HARD or a SOFT problem. That is, you have to identify the *kind* of issue that you're confronting.

HARD problems are issues to which you have to **react**. They are "givens." They are those conditions over which you have very little

> "Wisdom has two parts: Having a lot to say, and not saying it."
>
> —Author unknown

control. For example, they could involve your Family's relations in the context of the community or part of the country in which you live. Another *hard issue* would be the social acceptability of your lifestyle in the context of the city, county, or state in which you live. In the business world, *hard problems* concern such things as the political leadership out of Washington, laws, market constraints, product manufacturing, etc. Legal or health care issues sometimes arise that may have a bearing on where you reside.

SOFT problems, then, are those over which you *do* have quite a bit of choice and control. For example, whether or not you speak French is a *soft problem* because you can alter the answer by taking courses that teach you to speak French. Similarly, getting *more education* or gaining *additional skills* are both **soft problems.** Yes, they involve a lot of time and money—but I keep going over that point: *desires can be expensive.*

Amplify the problem; get better data—whether a hard or a soft problem:
- Who **says** it's a problem? Who wants it fixed?
- **How** do you measure this problem?
- **What is** that measurement now?
- What do you want that measurement to be **now and over time?**
- What is the **value to your Family of the difference** between what it is now and what you want it to be?
- **Who** or **what else** is affected?

Create a list of the kinds of results you would like to see for each of these problems. This becomes part of the goal-setting process. The relevant aphorism is: *What gets written down gets done.* The key is to concentrate on the effects of the problem, not on the problem, itself.

Build a new range of options for introducing the idea into your Family.

Build support for your idea.

Make distinctions:
- Perceived problem vs. the *real* problem
- Accepted problem vs. underlying causes/issues
- Political expediency vs. tough alternatives

Exercises such as this can help to strengthen your M/s relationship by bringing clarity to the larger issues that surround your relationship, or by clarifying issues that you think may inhibit your relationship from growing or moving into other dimensions. For example, you may fear/assume that some external force or condition is somehow limiting you or your Family. Discussing it and mapping the dimensions of the situation is likely to reveal some heretofore hidden options and opportunities.

The second part of this section concerns **performance problems.** This is the section you want to consider if your problem concerns your slave's behavior in some way. My all-time favorite book for separating performance problems is: *Analyzing Performance Problems: Or, You Really Oughta Wanna—How to Figure out Why People Aren't Doing What They Should Be, and What to do About It* by Robert Mager and Peter Pipe. About the best I can do, here, is to reproduce part of their table of contents—as I so strongly recommend you purchase the book.

I want to start this section with an admonition. If you think your problem deals with the performance of your slave, consider this...

Often, the problem with performance problems is that they are not what they at first appear to be. Not by a long shot. The slave's failure to do "X" *really means* "Y"..., or "K" or "B." What it *really* means may not be easily or logically derived. The slave may not be doing "X" because of an emotional hurt that will take some probing to reveal. That said, here is a start at a structure for teasing the situation apart.

Remember, this material comes from the table of contents of the Mager and Pipe book (tailored to the subject matter of this book, of course).

Is your partner not doing what he/she should be doing? What is the performance discrepancy? (Quantify the problem; explain to your partner why you care about this.)

- Specifically, how does the problem manifest itself now?
- How long has it been a problem?
- Who is affected and why do they care?
- How will you know if you're successful in fixing it?

Is it worth pursuing? Some issues don't rise to the level of even being a problem. In some cases, you may wish to wait for a better moment before discussing a behavior that you want modified. It's not that you're *hiding a problem*; it's that the particular issue isn't worth addressing at that time and/or would trigger a defensive reaction from the slave.

Let me speak for a minute on what is called *approximated behavior*. For our purposes, *approximated behavior* is behavior exhibited by your slave that is *on the right path* to exhibiting the behavior you seek, but not the *exact, precise* behavior you seek. Because your slave has to learn quite a bit of new behavior in order to mesh successfully and seamlessly with your life, you are bound to go through a period where little things *just aren't quite right*. Here, you have two choices: keep picking on the little issues; ignore the little issues.

The problem with picking on the unwanted behavior is that you risk pissing off your slave and giving him/her the idea that you are unreasonably (compulsively) picky. The other alternative is to say to yourself, as Master: "Look, I've accepted this person as my slave, and this is what I have to work with right now. Let me cherish this slave while he/she learns all my preferences and protocols. As the slave masters one set of duties/functions, I'll just add another set—*incrementally*." The key to making this work for you will be to set clear **priorities** with your slave about those preferences and protocols that you want mastered first, and then those that can be mastered later.

Explore fast fixes—there are likely to be some quick ways to solve the problem right away. For example, might you explain the rule or the procedure more clearly? Might you change or eliminate the rule? Within your M/s relationship, the key question is: "Is this rule or procedure serving Master, or has it become obsolete?"

Are the *consequences* for the desired behavior *right side up?* Is the desired performance itself punishing? (It takes much longer to do it right.) Is the undesired performance rewarding? (It's simply easier not to mop the kitchen floor every night. The slave gets more time with you.)

Are there any consequences at all? This is a test of your Mastery and your commitment to the M/s relationship. As Master, you may choose to instruct your slave to leave certain evening tasks incomplete in order that the two of you can play. The key, though, lies in the consciousness of the choice. That is, there is a **VAST** difference between **the slave** simply leaving the evening dishes undone in order to be available to play with you, and **you instructing the slave** to leave the dishes undone in order to come and play with you. In the first instance, the slave appears to have acted willfully—making the decision to leave the dishes undone—rather than acting per your instruction.

Are there other causes for the undesired behavior? For example, is the problem a skill deficiency? Could your slave perform this task in the past? Is this skill used often? If you're answering "yes" to questions such as these, then the cure calls for more (or more focused) training. However, it may be that the task, itself, is too complex and needs to be simplified.

If some obstacles are remaining, then your questions take a different turn: Is the equipment that slave is being asked to use appropriate for the task? Are there a lack of funds to buy something?

The final question along this line of logic is this: Is the slave properly motivated to complete the task to your specifications?

Again, I urge you to purchase the book *Analyzing Performance Problems*—I consider it a core reading for someone concerned with Master/slave relations.

Chapter 7
M/s Relationships Require Thoughtfulness

Some opinions about M/s relationships

There are certain lessons one learns after living over a decade on both sides of a Master/slave structure. While I learned the basics of structure while serving as a Master, I learned quite a bit more about the realities of mastery by serving as a slave for the past four years. Over these past four years, I've noticed my own conference presentations change in subtle ways. This section summarizes my current thought about managing our kinds of authority-based relationships.

Sustain your NRE
Ah! New Relationship Energy. So tasty and so exciting!! Why doesn't it stick around? When NRE goes, where does it go? Can you get it back?

For many people, the first several months of a new relationship are characterized by a wild emotional high. The new Master or slave is heaven-sent. The new partner is the most amazing surprise you've ever had. The new partner does everything perfectly. The new partner is so smart, so talented, so wise. The new partner, the new partner, the new partner. Jay Wiseman (author of *SM-101: A Realistic Introduction*) tells me that in polyamorous circles, this is known NRE—New Relationship Energy: he calls it the three-month crazies. Your task, during this period, is to discern whether the attraction is real or whether it's hormones. The phenomenon is well known; that's why most of us who have done this for a few weeks will advise you to *slow down*. Take it easy. Don't rush. Get to know the person as a person. That's why training contracts are often 3-4 months long. You have to see how the new partner looks and behaves in **six** months. Sex is great: give them a four-month sex contract. Hold off on the M/s stuff until you and they settle down.

The early stages of your relationship can be compared to a flight of stairs leading to a landing. As you're climbing the stairs, you're assessing one another. This is the period leading to your first decision point: that you're going to continue the relationship and not just keep it in the "friends" zone. Master's ability to use this period to test management and learning styles and to actively plan and mold the relationship gives slave an opportunity to assess how special Master considers this relationship to be. Is this a fuckfest or is it a time of learning?

The first plateau comes after the three-month crazies end. The job interview is over. You're feeling safe enough to reveal who you really are. Now you have to assess whether it's the person or the excitement of the new love that is keeping you interested? If you're genuinely interested in the relationship, how do you express that interest?

After some time, months for some couples, years for others, you'll reach *The Plateau*. The plateau represents a danger zone. This is the point you reach after you've declared yourselves to be a couple. There are no more secrets between you. You're happy with what you've built. However, you've now run through your easy conversation topics and one or both of you are sensing a kind of lack of obvious forward movement. Your relationship isn't going anywhere.

This is where the real work begins. This is where you risk recreating past relationships and past relationship problems with this new person. This is where you must deal with the purpose, intent, and meaning of your M/s dynamic. One of the central questions is: *how is this M/s relationship different from the two of you being together in a vanilla relationship*?

Some couples work very hard to keep NRE going throughout their lives. They adopt the attitude that yesterday is irretrievably gone and tomorrow isn't here yet, so they focus intently on the present. For people who do this, every day is the first and last day of their lives. Every day is infused with NRE. You're going to take a shower? Take it together. You're going to go out to dinner? Call ahead to reserve a romantic table. You're driving somewhere together? Hold hands in the car as one of you is driving. Master may assign slave the task of researching romance and related topics and presenting plans for keeping romance alive in the relationship.

Why am I walking you down this path? Because of the *Coolidge Effect*. The "Coolidge Effect" says, essentially, that we're drawn to new and sparkly things. It's just the way humans (particularly men) are biologically wired. New = different = interesting = brain-chemical release = altered judgment and behavior. In plain English: it's the tendency to want to fuck anything that walks. One of the effective antidotes is to keep your own relationship new and sparkly: keep the NRE going.

"So," you ask: "If we lose it how can we get it back?" Here are some ideas for you:

Write out what you have together as a couple...
- Five reasons you were attracted to this person in the first place.
- Five reasons you just LOVE being with this person once you're living together.
- Five special things (activities, protocols, rituals) that you used to do that have fallen away over time.
- Five kinds of entertainment that you both enjoy.

On the slightly negative side, write out...
- Five topics that are *off limits* for discussions because they get you guys in some kind of turmoil.
- Five things you've requested from your partner that they have not given you.
- Three places you've asked to go but your partner isn't interested in going.

Define what you each want...
- In order to *get it back* it helps to be conscious about what "it" is that your partner offers you which others cannot offer you.

- Inventory your blessings—actually write out how blessed you are to have this person as your partner.
- Separately, write out your top 8 needs in a partner, then compare lists. Are you a perfect match or only an okay match? Warning: if you're not very, very close to a perfect match, you know the areas you have to work on. In my experience, the areas that the other partner can NOT fulfill for you can balloon into relationship-ending issues.
- Check your purpose and intent: what are you as a couple; why are you a couple?
  - Are both of you seeking the same thing? (Be careful about words and word meanings: word interpretation can change as a function of personal baggage and upbringing. You may need to do some large-scale values clarification to be sure you're on the same page.)

Develop ways to celebrate your partnership...
- Remember, a *celebration* to one person may not be a celebration to the other; you have to agree upon what a celebration even represents for each of you.
- Build intimate protocols that isolate stressful discussions or stressful times to avoid contaminating the entire relationship. Develop personal relationship protocols that seal off the stresses of daily life from the magic of who you are together. (Consider establishing a bathing ritual or other rituals that seal off the day's worries from the few high-quality hours you have at night to be together.)
- Recognize that while this may not be the first time you are doing something, it IS the first time that you are doing these things today.
  - Remember the excitement of holding hands, kissing the nape of her neck, cuddling during a rainy day (you can play a CD of rain and thunder in the background and cuddle up on the couch and watch a movie—we do!).
  - Consider how your home or your bedroom support or detract from your intent to be in a loving and exciting relationship with your partner. (Do some research into *anchors* and *pre-trance states* and learn to use these

to set your living space up to support *romance* in your relationship)

- Show that you've been thinking of your partner when you are apart.
- Develop supportive household protocols (wear *house uniform*; use the process of cleaning dishes/house to be mindful of your M/s dynamic: bring purpose and mindfulness to mundane activities).
- Find ways to stay in touch throughout the day: send texts and emails to each other; if possible, call one another a time or two during the day.

Authority-based relationships are a lot of work: they are *not vanilla*. They offer an opportunity to have a relationship unlike 99% of other relationships in the world.

But, it's up to you both to bring this kind of energy into your lives. Nobody will do it for you.

Focus: don't *drift*

As Master Jim Glass says: "Decisions in this relationship always serve the Family's wellbeing."

Unlike a vanilla relationship, a Leather Master/slave structured relationship is serving a higher purpose. As Master, it is incumbent upon you to keep that vision in the forefront of your mind and behavior. You have much more to do in this kind of relationship than you would have to do in a husband/wife relationship.

In the same way that a Master/slave relationship is based on structure, you may—like me—find it extremely helpful to put more thought and structure into your lives as a couple (or threesome, or more).

As Lewis Carroll said in *Alice in Wonderland*, "If you have no destination, any road will take you there."

This brings up the point about not *drifting* into your future.

I'm completely committed to thinking through where I want to be in five or ten or twenty years, and then focusing my energies towards that goal. I've found that to be very successful. The more clearly I can explain my goals and work through the necessary steps to attain the goals, the more easily my new life unfolds before me. There are many planning models you can use to build a personal/Family plan: pick one and use it. Here is a very basic (and well-established) model that works well for individuals or small businesses that don't have a lot of strategic planning experience:

Identify your purpose (mission statement). This is the statement (or statements) that describe why your Family exists, i.e., its basic purpose. What are you and your slave all about? Are you focusing primarily on yourselves and your relationship, or are you intending to give something back to the Community? If you intend to give back, what are you giving back? Time? Service? Money? Wisdom? The statements will change somewhat over the years.

Select the goals your Family must reach to accomplish its mission. Goals are general statements about what you need to accomplish to meet your purpose, or mission, and they address major issues/constraints that you will face in the process.

Identify specific approaches or strategies that must be implemented to reach each goal. Strategies often change quite a bit as the Family eventually conducts more robust strategic planning, particularly by more closely examining what are called the **external** and **internal** environments of the Family. An external environment concerns outside forces that have an impact on your Family. The internal environment concerns itself with how the two (or three or four…) of you have learned to interact and work together.

Identify specific action plans to implement each strategy. These are the specific job responsibilities that each member must undertake to ensure effective implementation of each strategy. Objectives should be clearly worded to the extent that people can assess if the objectives have or have not been met. Ideally, each type of job function within the Family would have a work plan, or set of objectives. For example, if one objective is to develop a House Protocols book, that project would have its own action plan. If one objective is to improve the Family's wardrobe, that objective would have its own action plan. Ditto if the objective was to obtain new training in order to obtain a better job in order to bring more money into the Family.

Monitor and update the plan. Business planners regularly reflect on the extent to which the goals are being met and whether action plans are being implemented. Perhaps the most important indicator of Family success comes from comments by friends who notice positive changes in your life.

Tips about bringing in a "third"
Baby steps to polyamory

So: you want to move your monogamous relationship into poly. Communication is the secret. Time tends to become an issue.

One thing to consider is to begin to spend time apart.

Have partner A stay home while partner B goes out and vice versa.

When you're apart, how much information do you need about what the other person is doing? Do you need to know what they are doing, who they are with, etc, or only that they are having fun?

If you view the time apart as a chance for your partner to have fun and a chance for you to do something that you want to do (or to have alone time) then you'll look forward to the separation rather than dreading it.

Emotions in relationships

Clearly a truism, there are substantial differences between men and women raised in Western civilization when it comes to accessing and expressing emotions. Thus, it will also be a truism that the emotional structure of an M/s relationship in the Western world will feel quite different, depending upon the gender structure:

- male Master, male slave;
- male Master, female slave;
- female Master, female slave;
- female Master, male slave.

Yes, I know it's not this simple—but you get the idea.

People vary in the degree to which they can access and rely upon their own emotions. Some people tend mostly to think about their relationships with others; other people tend more easily to feel their relationships with others. When stress enters the M/s relationship, these differences can become exaggerated. I encourage you to explore relationship differences; there are many great books out there and I've found them extremely helpful. Some suggested readings are:

- John Gray, *Men Are from Mars, Women Are from Venus: The Classic Guide to Understanding the Opposite Sex*. New York, NY: HarperCollins, 1992.
- Gary D. Chapman, *The Five Love Languages: How to Express Heartfelt Commitment to Your Mate*. Northfield Publishing; Reissue edition, 1995.

Side note: I suspect gender ties closely with the degree of emotional control expressed both by Master and by slave. I'd argue that a female Master will run a much more empathetic M/s dynamic than will a male master whose general viewpoint is that *might makes right*. This particularly comes into play when Master starts talking about the idea of expanding the Family to include multiple slaves or polyamorous sexual partners. Translation: I think that a discussion about multiple sex partners is going to be received differently by slaves of different genders. But, I could be wrong.

Some ways to think about *love*

The *love* topic is highly individualized: each couple has to approach it in their own way. Here are some summaries of the more vocal factions.

Everyone starts out in love. Well, you usually start out in lust, but you usually don't say that out loud. The in-love stage lasts anywhere from a few months to a few years and is characterized by both partners doing the best they can to overlook or to lessen the habits/behaviors of the other person that don't fit the fantasy image that they have created in their minds of how this other person should behave. And, both partners are having lots and lots of fun and hot sex during this stage. But this stage ends: either Master introduces some distancing in order to maintain authority, or slave introduces some distancing as they realize that this Master may not, in fact, be exactly right for them (and they don't know how to extract themselves).

Love is the steady-state emotion that takes over after the in-love stage wears out. This is probably the most commonly accepted viewpoint for love-based M/s (as opposed to service-based M/s). Many Masters feel that if they're going to put all the time and effort into training a slave with whom they will spend lots of time, they want to be submerged in a loving relationship with that person. Many slaves say that they'd never go through what they're going through if their Master didn't love them.

Some believe that love contaminates Master's ability to make emotionally-pure decisions. When the M/s relationship is based on service and obedience (as opposed to being based on amorous love), two issues come into play:
- whether Master's love for slave causes Master to limit the kinds of orders given to slave;
- whether slave is complying with an order out of *love* or out of *obedience*. (Since obedience is the core of the M/s dynamic, Master would lose the capacity to monitor the slave's core reactions.)

There is love *and then there is* **love**. The word, itself, represents a concept, not a practice. The way 16-year-olds explain love is a world apart from how 60-year-olds explain it. Your own understanding of love changes as you gain more personal experience. Suffice it to say, loving M/s relationships differ substantially from girlfriend/boyfriend relationships, as the latter do not involve the power exchange or authority transfer inherent in D/s and M/s structures.

There can be substantial differences between Master's love and slave's love. The Master is more likely to love the slave—rather than be *in love* with the slave. The slave is more likely to fall *in love* with Master. This situation, where the Master "loves" the slave and the slave is "in love" with the Master can lead to some potential misunderstandings and stress unless discussed openly and with truthfulness. It may be useful to discuss different forms of love with a prospective slave, lest they confuse your relationship.

Love is sometimes described as having three elements. If you start doing research into "love," you almost immediately realize that the Greeks had this figured out in great detail a few years ago. I'll summarize the Greek analysis of the word, as in English it's almost too broadly applied to be useful.

The Greeks divided love into three or four elements depending upon which research paper you're reading: I'm going to use the three-element approach in this book. The three elements are as follows:

- Eros: Eros is amorous love that covers everything from queasy stomachs and warm fuzzy feelings to strong sensual passion. Eros has two characteristics. First, it's situation-specific. If you're having a good time, you've got *eros*, but any hurtful word or deed will cause it to evaporate. Second, it's perception-based. If you, yourself, perceive a setting to be romantic, it is. However, the minute your partner articulates that they don't think it's romantic, your perception will shift and *eros* will (again) evaporate.
- Philia: Philia is the love of friendship, best friends, and the fellowship of being with those people you enjoy. *Philia* love can have limitations and conditions that have the ability to break the love because of unforgiven hurt.
- Agape: Unlike the previous two types of love, *agape* is not limited to being held hostage by its environment and someone's perception. *Agape* is based upon the commitment of a decision. It entails the decision to proactively seek someone's well-being.

Now to the point of all this: imagine this graph as a triangle. You can put your finger on any of the three points or anywhere inside the triangle.

Since *love* is really a combination of some amount of each of these concepts, by putting your finger somewhere inside the triangle, you can graphically represent the kind of love you feel towards someone. In the most general way, and from the s-type's perspective, an M/s structure that is based on love is mostly of the eros variety while love an M/s structure that is based on service and obedience is mostly of the agape variety.

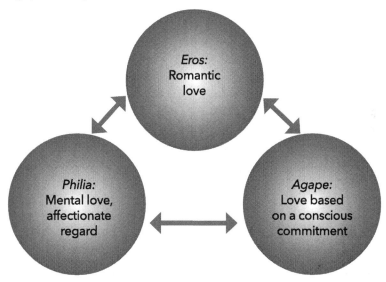

Mindfulness, purpose, and intent

This is one of the sections of this book where you're likely to get part way into it and stop, hold the book out in front of yourself and ask: "Is this really a book about forming Master/slave relationships?

Yup.

Perhaps the characteristic of M/s relationships that sets them so far apart from others is that we can use this strong structure to remake ourselves and/or to focus on improving our relationships with others. At its core, M/s relationships—as many of us practice them—are about *purposefulness*.

I've only run into discussions such as you're about to read when attending Master/slave conferences and attend workshops on relationships. I've selected some of my more favorite topics to share with you in this book.

Trust me: every one of these points come into play whether you are striving to be an outstanding Master or an outstanding slave.

Agreements

If you're going to hold someone *accountable*, you have to be sure that they are aware of the areas for which they are being held accountable. Over the years, I have come to use *structured agreements* for things that matter. I do this because the forced structure of an Agreement makes the communication particularly clear. As I use them, *Agreements* have four components:

- State the offer/acceptance (I agree…).
- Specify the general item to be done (…to wash the outside of the car…).
- List conditions of satisfaction—be clear about the level of activity (…so that all of the dirt and tar are completely removed and no water spots remain…).
- Specify the time frame (…within the next two hours).

If the slave suspects that he/she cannot fully accomplish any of the four aspects of the Agreement, the slave must respectfully decline to agree to it, and then explain the reticence (in our case, I have usually forgotten that my slave is already working on another task and this new task presents a conflict with my own Instructions). The modification of any aspect of the Agreement **must** be done BEFORE the Agreement is accepted or as soon as the need for modification becomes apparent.

If the slave has made an Agreement and later discovers that he/she may be unable to complete it on time, it is VERY IMPORTANT to contact Master and discuss the situation *before the time period expires*.

Failure to keep an Agreement will carry Consequences.

In my world, Agreements are a big deal. I don't use them casually. I don't mind modifying an agreement at the front end; I don't even mind being contacted regarding a change to the deadline. However, I mind a great deal if no effort was made to renegotiate the terms and conditions of an Agreement, and it is not fulfilled exactly as it was set forth.

Because I am so focused on keeping Agreements perfectly, I cautioned my slave not to enter lightly into a formal Agreement with me. I'm going to be easier to get along with if the slave says: "Master, with respect, Sir, I cannot fulfill the terms you are proposing, Sir," rather than entering into an Agreement suspecting that the terms cannot be fulfilled.

I will comment further on this point. I've known people who would agree to do just about anything with little or no intention of doing so. I had a professor who would promise anything just to get you to go away. While it seemed that he was being cooperative and helpful, he was simply being manipulative. Aware of my personal sensitivity concerning this point—that I will aggressively challenge any failure to keep an Agreement—I explain *how to manage Agreements* to those who work closely with me. Similarly, on those occasions that I feel an Agreement is needed to accomplish some significant task, I'm careful to review the component parts of the Agreement and remind the slave of the importance of communicating changes to me **ahead of time**.

Time

For many (including myself), *time* is important. It's one of the most valuable assets a person possesses. After all, when you run out of time, you're called *dead*. Since you don't quite know when you will run out of time, you might consider making every day important. Personally, I view an M/s relationship as an ideal opportunity to examine your relationship with… *time*. Do you both look at *time* the same way? Stephen Hawking, in his book *A Brief History of Time* mentions that in a general way, people look at time in one of two ways. Some people view time as a flowing river; if you don't get something done today there is always tomorrow. Others, though, view time as linear: you can run out of it. Hawking says that for better or worse, people with these nearly polar views of time tend to pair up. In an M/s setting, that can mean that one person tells the other person to be at a certain place at 3pm but the other person *hears* that as: be at a certain place around

3pm. Fights result. I'm bringing this up so you can speak about it within your own relationship.

In addition to the philosophical underpinnings, *time commitments* represent a daily opportunity to keep your word. They are a form of Agreement. If the slave has been told an arrival or departure time, Master expects that time to be honored with precision. There will be Consequences to violating time issues—not the least of which is having to put up with my reaction to the slave being late.

Keeping one's word is a core concept within the Leather culture. From the very beginning of my exposure to the Leather World, I was struck by the degree of honesty, integrity, and high moral purpose I found there. If a Leatherman says something will be done, you can be sure it will be. If I, as Master, have told someone that I will arrive at a certain time, tardiness by my slave will NOT cause me to be late to that meeting. If my slave is not ready to leave on time, I will leave without her and attend to her consequences later.

Principles of a good relationship
- You can't expect to have what you want if you don't ask for what you want
- Just because you feel bad doesn't necessarily mean someone did something wrong
- Just because you feel good doesn't necessarily mean what you're doing is right
- Integrity matters
- Expectation on your part does not incur obligation on someone else's
- When you feel something scary or unpleasant, talk about it
- While there may be good reasons for not saying something at a particular time, if the only reason that you're holding back is out of some unidentified fear, then perhaps you need to say it
- Your partners add value to your life; treat them preciously
- Make sure your partner's heart is safe in your hands
- The easiest way to FIND someone with the qualities you like is to be someone that a person with those qualities finds interesting
- People are not commodities; they are never interchangeable

- Your partner will do many things that are Not About You
- Different people express love differently; learn to recognize the way others express and receive love
- Don't treat people the way you'd have them treat you; treat them the way they'd have you treat them
- Pay attention
- We are born of frailty and error, and must forgive one another's failings
- Being in a relationship that does not meet your needs is not necessarily better than being alone
- Love is abundant
- It is not necessary to be the best at everything, or even anything; you alone bring your unique mix of qualities to the table
- Relationships that are consciously chosen are usually more rewarding than relationships built on default assumptions
- Don't play games, especially with other people's hearts
- Relationships are often different in theory than in practice
- Be flexible
- A sense of humor will get you through times of no sanity better than sanity will get you through times of no humor
- A partner who chooses to be with you is more satisfying than a partner who can't leave
- Real security comes from within
- People are not need fulfillment machines
- Don't look to others to complete you
- Life is Change
- Sometimes you will feel uncomfortable; that's normal, and not something to be feared
- All of us are lousy at predicting how we will feel in new circumstances
- When you hurt someone—and you will—suck it up, take responsibility, and do what you can to make it right
- Relationships end; it doesn't mean they were a failure, or that your ex-partners are bad people
- Your heart will, at some point, be broken, and that's okay; you will survive, and find love again
- Feelings are not fact
- Fear of intimacy is the enemy of happiness
- Compassion is most necessary when it's most difficult

- Don't vilify those who hurt you; they are people, too
- It is possible for two people to deeply, profoundly love each other but not be good life partners
- Being uncomfortable is not, in itself, a reason not to do something
- You can't be generous or compassionate when you fear loss
- The world is as it is, not as we want it to be
- Life's song is filled with beauty and chaos and joy and sorrow and pain and uncertainty and ecstasy and heartache and passion; to fear any of these things is to fear life
- Treat those you love with respect
- Life rewards people who move in the direction of greatest courage

Habits of calmness

These are the habits to develop that will help you develop calmness (based on my experience):

A calm morning ritual. Mornings are busy times and our days are filled with things to do. I get it. We go to work, we take care of Master or slave, and we manage the House and its upkeep. However, every bit of wisdom about being a happy person and about directing your own life urges you to set time aside daily to express your gratitude: gratitude for those close to you and gratitude for being able to hear birds chirp and leaves rustle in the wind. I'd urge you to create a formal daily ceremony to enable you to become centered and express your gratitude; ceremony will help you with this process. The rest of your day will benefit. Those who live and work around you will benefit.

Learn to watch your response. The world happens around you. You're driven to action over some things; you're driven to tears over others. Some incidents anger you; others overwhelm you. The thing of it is, your emotions are running away with your mind. If you'd like a high-impact self-help course on taking control of your emotions, I'd recommend Tom Miller's audio course: *Self-Discipline and Emotional Control.* It gives you the tools to take back your "rider" from your "horse." Your mind is the rider, the horse is your *lizard brain*—your emotional reaction to life's events. It's a great course. It teaches you how to watch your responses—it's an important habit.

Don't take things personally. Many times your responses are triggered because you've taken things personally. If someone does something we don't like, often we tend to interpret this as a personal affront. Our slave hasn't kept the closet clean? They are defying us! slave has not done something he/she was supposed to? He/she is showing resistance! Some people lose sight of the reality that the other person is simply dealing with their own personal issues: they're doing the best they can. You can learn not to interpret events as a personal affront, and instead see it as some non-personal external event (like a leaf falling, a bird flying by) that you can either respond to without a stressful mindset, or not need to respond to at all. If this paragraph sings to you, I'd strongly urge you to check out Gary van Warmerdam's course *Pathway to Happiness*. I've found it to be incredibly helpful in life. Well worth the money.

Be grateful. The purpose of gratitude is to make us aware and present in our lives, to teach us not to take anything for granted. After all, you or I could be killed or maimed in a car crash tomorrow. It's easy to get caught up in our daily life and overlook the good things that are part of our environment. Actively practicing acts of gratitude enables us to reconnect with how unbelievably fortunate we are to be alive in this day and age, living in the country that we do, able to participate in a relationship lifestyle that in most parts of the world would cause us to be shunned. As corny as it sounds, you might consider starting every day with the question: *What am I grateful for today?* See, the first step to changing your life wasn't that painful right? Common sense, you can totally do this! Oh—and then smile. This unbending habit can change your life.

Create stress-coping habits. We often have unhealthy responses when faced with stress: anger, withdrawing because we feel overwhelmed, eating junk food, consuming alcohol or drugs, buying stuff, wasting time on the Internet, procrastinating, and so on. But—if you're reading this book, you're either walking down a path to Mastery or to slavery. In either case, you're marching to the beat of a drummer on a very different level than in the world of vanillas. You have the opportunity to recognize that you're in control of yourself and your reactions to events. You have the opportunity to develop coping-responses that fit our own personality. I'm not about to list stress-coping strategies—you have to do your own legwork, here: what works for me isn't likely to work for you. I'm a 70-year old het male. You're not that.

Single-tasking: I know: we've all grown up being taught that multi-tasking is good. For medical proof, just look at cardiovascular disease in developed countries. Look at suicide rates in Japan or among teenagers. Look at auto accident statistics. It doesn't work. Multi-tasking causes a level of anxiety that runs through everything you do, because you're always worried you should be doing more, doing something else. What if, instead, you just did one thing, and learned to trust that you shouldn't be doing anything else? It takes practice: just eat. Just wash your bowl. Just walk. Just talk to someone. Just read one article or book without switching. Just write. Just do your e-mail, one at a time, until your inbox is empty. You'll learn that there is peace in just doing one thing, and letting go of everything else. Perhaps you might consider exploring Taoism or Buddhism... I'm just sayin'...

Reduce noise. Our lives are filled with all kinds of noise — visual clutter, notifications, social media, news, all the things we need to read. And truthfully, none of it is necessary. Reduce all these things and more, and create some space, some quiet, in your life.

Beliefs about life and people

A substantial proportion of the leaders in the Leather M/s movement discuss the importance of the spiritual aspects of their relationships and actions. This represents another topic that, for many, will require serious thought. The spiritual aspect is important for a variety of reasons. For example, it concerns the *purpose* of your SM play. Are you *flogging* your slave because you like the feeling or the process, or because *flogging* represents a path to spiritual and cathartic release? Think about the slave candidate you're playing with...when you are finished *playing*, does he/she get up and thank you for your skill and technique, or does this person lie there virtually motionless for 20-30 minutes, overwhelmed by the magic that has just enveloped him or her? It's not that one scene is inherently better than the other—just that they are *different*. Have you ever thought about BDSM practices as being a *vehicle* to take your partner to a *different plane*? Have you ever tried to grapple with what it *is the* two of you do together that is so *special*?

Let's move now from spiritual beliefs to beliefs about people. It's not important that you agree or disagree with these bulleted points. The issue is: *how do you react to these statements*? By considering the statements that elicit emotional responses, you may learn something about how you—and your slave—are wired.

(NOTE: Let me be clear–these may or may not be my own personal views; I'm just presenting a collection of attitudes that I've heard people express over the years.)

- People? There's nobody out there other than who you create (or recreate) when you go out in the world. Even then, you can only see that person through your own psychological filters. Your version of "George Washington" is so different from George Washington's version of "George Washington" that there is not likely to be much common ground beyond a physical description that has come down to us from a portrait of the artist's version of him.
- People are inherently good, kind, and loving; you just have to give them a chance.
- People are only *civilized* out of fear of being caught and exposed. Everyone would rape, murder, and steal, if they thought they could get away with it.
- Every person has worth. Even a rapist, con artist, or burglar has worth. You must be able to forgive the person who kills your child.
- If people meet your expectations, you'll like them and let them be your friend. Violate your values, and you'll cast them out forever.
- You believe everyone until they give you reason not to trust or believe them.
- Thin as a rail; no meat on her/his bones. He/she must be overly controlling and compulsive; no joy in this one—probably an introvert. You're just not interested.
- Sloppy body, sloppy mind. If the person doesn't care enough about him/herself to stay thin and trim. You're just not interested.
- While you can be polite to almost anyone, a person would

have to be very special for you to be willing to give them your time or attention. You don't do *normal people* very well.

- You just love people. Big, tall, short, small. You revel in their aliveness; they all have such interesting stories to tell.
- You believe that people have been put on earth to see one another through, not to see through one another.

As you can well imagine, someone who thinks they *recreate people in the world* every time they go out is going to have a dramatically different relationship with people than the person who believes that everyone is inherently good, kind, and loving, or the person who believes that everyone is a rapist at heart.

So, a project: Sit down with your potential partner and work out your beliefs about people. Caveat: you may have trouble actually admitting—or getting your partner to admit—true sentiments on this score. The reason is that if your views are not personally flattering (socially acceptable), you aren't likely to reveal them. Similarly, your partner may be less than honest on this same score.

This, then, forces you back into the world of social science research. You are going to have to work out proxy measures for this topic. Remember: a *proxy measure* is an unrelated—but acceptable—question you can ask that actually answers another question. For example, if you wanted to explore someone's views on self-determination, you might ask some questions about their reactions to street beggars—the homeless.

- How do you think that person got there?
- Do you give money to street people?
- Have you ever considered volunteering at a Salvation Army center or the like?
- Can you imagine ever becoming homeless? Does that frighten you?
- How would you feel about inviting a homeless person to come home with us for a good meal? Well, then how about fixing a nice dinner for someone and driving around until you find the first street person and presenting it to him or her?
- What would you say about spending next weekend doing volunteer service downtown with the XYZ Center?

I suspect that you'll learn a lot about your partner's empathy quotient, while you'll also learn their attitudes about work ethics, cleanliness, fate, and deistic determinism.

Awareness

Reactance and resistance

Reactance is thoughtless: you don't think, you react. A reaction may, in fact, be contrary to your own underlying wishes or beliefs, but it just pops out. It's accidental. It's instinctive.

Resistance is willful. You've made a specific decision that you're going to resist whatever issue or order is on the table.

Sooner or later, you are going to encounter reactance *and* resistance from your slave. It's simply inevitable if you're living together. You give an order; your slave reacts to the order. This reaction can take the form of a look of defiance, a little expression of exasperation or disgust, a rolling of eyes, or a direct challenge that questions the order.

Perhaps the most common low-level problem occurs when the slave reacts with some vanilla-sounding reply such as: "Oh, sure. I'll go get it." The problem with a reply of this sort is that it is not mindful: it is not respecting either the relationship or the power imbalance between slave and Master. In these situations, you might consider saying something to the effect of: "And how would that reply be phrased if you were in protocol?" That is generally enough to get the slave to recognize the lapse and to restate the sentence as: "Sir, yes Sir! I'll go get it, Sir."

But, stepping up the scale, the time will come when you issue an order and the slave reacts to it in a way that you feel must be addressed; that your failure to address the issue will degrade the nature of the authority exchange upon which the relationship is based. In such a case, I recommend you consider what is called a *state change*. Here, you stop whatever is going on at the time and change both your physical position and your slave's physical position. You may consider declaring a "time out" so you can each separate and cool down before the "discussion" edges into a blow-up. You may consider tightening down control in some way or another. You might consider using talking sticks to get the emotion out of the discussion (you can look the procedure up online).

This is a time for both Master and slave to refocus and discuss:
- What happened?
- How did you react?
- What was good and bad about that reaction?
- How would you do it differently next time?

A Master with an open mind and open heart will learn a great deal at this point—often about himself/herself, rather than about the slave.

Reactance, unaddressed, is likely, at some point, to become resistance. **Resistance** occurs when the submissive/slave resists Master's dominance—sometimes unconsciously. Now, you've got a problem. This is likely to be a substantial signal that something fundamental is amiss. This requires some careful probing and questioning. In my experience, when a slave gets to the point of demonstrating resistance, Master is being inattentive—Master is not hearing/seeing/feeling the slave's signals for help/relief on some front. Again, my continual theme: you need outstanding listening skills and an appreciation of the world through the slave's eyes.

Visible and invisible knowledge

I consider this topic to be **extremely important** when two people are working together—particularly if one person is asking the other to *do something* or to *get something*. YOU know some things that your slave **doesn't** know; your slave knows some things that **you** don't know. Some categories of knowledge (often gender-linked because of the way we are brought up in the US) are simply invisible to the other person. Some examples:
- If you're used to doing your own plumbing, you'll get this right away: you're under the sink working on a repair. You have two large pipe wrenches at your elbow, but you've forgotten your gunk (or calking tape). You ask your slave to run to the garage and to bring you a tube of calking compound (or calking tape)

plus a two-inch crescent wrench. Your slave doesn't move. Nothing. Blank stare. You might as well have spoken in Greek. A two-inch crescent wrench and calking tape are not items your partner knows about.

- You'll get this right away if you're used to doing your own shopping: you gave Master a shopping list of items to pick up at the grocery store (go with me on this one—he wanted to go to the store anyway). You say: "Master, when you go out for the wine, would you please bring back a nice steak for tonight's dinner?" "Sure," he says and walks out the door. An hour later, he comes back with a *choice* grade of *sirloin*. You blanch: how could he do this?! This was to be a special dinner; he knew this. You'd brought flowers home the night before that he knew were for tonight's table; as he had been leaving he'd seen you putting fresh candles on the table! You had even discussed the type of Cabernet he was going out to pick up right now! How could he come home with a choice sirloin?? You *assumed* he knew to buy a **prime fillet,** perhaps a ribeye, or at worst, a NY strip steak; you *assumed he knew* that you ONLY buy a prime cut when you're dressing up at home for this kind of dinner. How could this happen? If he was confused, why didn't he simply call you from the store? When you delicately ask Master about it, he explains that it was the right *shape* for the steaks you always buy. "Shape!!?" you think to yourself; "What's *shape* got to do with it?" Disconnect: invisible knowledge. The *grade* and *cut* of the meat didn't mean anything—only the *shape* of the meat.

Not only are there many areas that are blind from one gender to another—having something to do with how boys and girls are socialized—but also there are knowledge and experience gaps between social classes. For example, if you're in a truck stop, *chatting with the waitress* is perfectly normal. Ditto if you're at national chain restaurants where waiters are hired without much experience. The waitperson is likely to be chatty as a way of making larger tips. Not a problem. However, if you're in an elite restaurant with linen service where two waiters have been assigned to your table and you start speaking with the professional waitperson, you immediately telegraph that you're clueless about social etiquette. In this case, conversing with the wait staff is improper, and your host is going to draw many conclusions about you from that gaffe.

Coming around very gingerly to the topic of *social etiquette*, and *visible and invisible knowledge*, and *unconscious incompetence*, I'll give you a concrete example that ties back to slave training. Depending upon the person's upbringing—gender won't matter, here—some people bend at the waist when bending over in a kitchen (or elsewhere) to remove something from a low storage cabinet. Those with a more careful upbringing will squat—in order that their rear-ends not stick out. This degree of personal behavior is invisible to most people and will telegraph your upbringing. (So will the way you sit down on a chair or couch, by the way.)

One message, then, is that it will benefit your relationship if both of you are sensitive to the different sets of assumptions that have resulted from differences in your backgrounds. The slave may be working as hard as he/she can and still seem to be *missing* important points that Master thinks are perfectly obvious. These points are only obvious once you know they exist.

During the training stage, Master must be able to distinguish between visible and invisible knowledge in order to know when to provide more training for your slave rather than to correct them.

The Four Stages of Learning
As I often point out, you have to be aware that an area of knowledge exists in order even to think about learning about it. After all, when you're a one-year-old, you don't know much more than that a few sounds that you make produce results that seem to satisfy you. You only have to consider how much you now know to appreciate how many ideas you've been exposed to throughout your life. But, did you ever stop to wonder *how* you learn new information? When starting a new job, have you ever considered how new skills or knowledge move from being invisible to you to being automatic for you?

The answer is that in a general way, there are four stages of developing competence in any field. Knowing about these four stages will help you to assess the amount of training you and/or your slave will need when you encounter a new idea.

Unconscious incompetence: You don't know something, but you don't really know that you don't know it.

Conscious incompetence: Though you don't understand some concept (or know how to do something), you recognize that some people do understand that thing (or know how to do it). Once you decide to learn something new, your learning involves making mistakes.

Conscious competence: You understand or know how to do something, but demonstrating the skill or knowledge requires concentration. The new skill or knowledge may be broken down into steps, and you may have to focus on each step in order to do it. (Put the key in the car's ignition; turn the car on; check the rear-view mirror…)

Unconscious competence: You have had so much practice with a skill that it has become second nature and you can perform it easily and without conscious thought. As a result, the skill can be performed while executing another task (driving and texting??). You have reached *understanding*, and you would now be able to teach that knowledge or skill to others.

Look: life in general—and successfully managing a Master/slave relationship in particular—involves a complex learning curve. The more you learn, the more you realize that there is a lot more to learn. Educated people have known this for eons. Here are the same concepts expressed elegantly as an ancient Oriental proverb:

He who knows not, and knows not that he knows not, is a fool; shun him.
(Unconscious Incompetent)

He who knows not, and knows that he knows not, is ignorant; teach him.
(Conscious Incompetent)

He who knows, and knows not that he knows, is asleep; wake him.
(Unconscious Competent)

He who knows, and knows that he knows, is a wise man; follow him.
(Conscious Competent)

By the way, for your amusement, here's the American version of this same observation courtesy of Baseball great Yogi Bera: "It's not what you don't know that gets you in trouble. It's what you know for sure that just ain't so."

So… when it comes to complex topics such as authority-imbalanced relationships, you're going to have to learn a lot before you can realize that you haven't yet learned very much. The number of little techniques and nuances are so great that you'll never master them all. In fact, you'll often be surprised how much a little communications technique can help you even if you've been a couple for many years.

Chapter 8
Endings

Up to this point, this book has discussed creating and maintaining an M/s relationship. I have not discussed ending such a relationship. Right now, I want to bring up a topic developed by my partner, Jen. It concerns the end of a relationship.

Starting with an exit strategy

In a marriage, the exit strategy is called divorce and the procedures are pretty well laid out. But, what if you're not married?

Yes, you hope that your M/s relationship will last forever, but so do people who are getting married. You can save a lot of anger and hurt if you discuss options for ending your relationship while you're still deeply in love. Interestingly, there are really two basic planning topics: being clear that you are, in fact, ending the relationship and doing so publically so you don't confuse your local community.

Let me explain.

Most break-ups are messy. One person usually feels left behind. Break-ups often trigger both an emotional and a financial crisis: the s-type may have to move at the same time that they're feeling abandoned by the person they loved. This can be devastating on their self-image. Worse, their BDSM friends are now concerned about how to treat these people who are no longer a couple: while as a couple they were often invited to parties, now—as two single people (or as one single person plus a newly partnered couple)—people aren't sure how to interact with either. How can you invite sub-sally to a party where her ex is now with a new partner? Worse, the person who was left may not yet have fallen out of love with their ex-partner. They're grieving. They're angry. They're hurt. Worse times two, sometimes the person doing the leaving tries to justify leaving by blaming their ex-sub; sometimes the person who was left decides that the best vindication is revenge and talks to anyone who will listen about what an $%*@#^ their ex is.

It doesn't have to be that way. You have some options that can help both of you through the emotional trauma if your relationship is heading for a break-up.

The best advice I can offer is: first, silly as it may sound, be clear that you are actually breaking up. Many relationships just fizzle out. Neither person really ends the thing, it's just that you're no longer living together. This makes it hard on both people and hard on your friends, as you both may yearn for the other but know better than to try to get back together. When you get to the next section, you'll find a few paragraphs that describe The Invisible Collar. I don't want to go into it here, but that phrase describes the lingering yearning people can feel over unresolved separations.

However, what *is* relevant for this section is the antidote not only for the invisible collar but also for personal and community upset: formalize your breakup. Have an *uncollaring* ceremony; end the thing in the eyes of your community. That way, you have a chance to remain friends with someone you have loved intensely. You're allowed to continue to love your ex-partner: loving someone and being able to live with that person are separate issues.

Don't be an asshole about your breakup. It won't help you feel better about yourself as a person and it won't help your reputation. Remember: your next potential partner is watching how you handle this breakup.

The Invisible Collar

My partner and co-author created the term *invisible collar* to describe the lingering emotional connection between people after an emotionally bonding experience that does not end decisively. It doesn't matter whether the emotionally bonding experience is a single intense scene or a months- or years-long intense personal relationship. What seems to matter is that there was not a clearly understood end.

She coined the phrase after recognizing some common patterns emerging from discussions about M/s relationship break-ups. In particular, Jen noticed that people who had been involved in intense relationships that had ended with closure reported very different post-relationship experiences than did people whose relationships had just fizzled away.

While *huge* emotional pain and trauma often come with the end of relationships, it seemed that people got over their break-ups much faster when those relationships had been ended with dignity and formality. In fact, many people admitted that when they had been in relationships that had ended without closure, they often felt a lingering connection that could last for many months or even years. During that agonizing time of unresolved separation, one or both of the previous partners would want to call/contact/reach out to the other person. Many people said they continued to think about the way the relationship had ended and wished that they could have done something differently to have prevented the break-up. These people reported that the other person was often on their mind and that this period was a slow emotional torture.

Jen coined the term *invisible collar* to describe the long-lasting tug (or pull) towards a prior relationship partner long after they had expected those feelings to go away. She and I discussed the concept quite a bit and realized that the *invisible collar* concept ties in with the way one ends a scene with people other than regular committed partners.
- You enter an interaction (either for a meeting, a scene, or even a brief relationship) with purpose and intent.

- When the meeting/scene/relationship is over, you either have or have not fulfilled your purpose and intent.
- To the extent that something is left unfinished, to the extent that you feel that the connection did not resolve completely, you may be left with a *psychological connection* that may take longer to fade than you expected.

That's the Invisible Collar.

And that's a wrap for this book.

I hope you have enjoyed reading this book as much as I have enjoyed writing it. While living it, I've also been studying this form of structured relationship for a number of years, reading widely in what literature I could find and attending M/s conferences that offered instructive seminars. I have learned a great deal by watching others work through their own relationship issues—and I am constantly striving to find ways to improve my own working relations with my partner.

Please feel free to contact me: I'm Dr_Bob on FetLife. You're welcome to send me a friend request. Also, let me know if you want to be added to the mailing list receive announcements when I come out with other books or will be attending conferences and such.

May the wind always be at your back.

Dr. Bob and M. Jen

Supplements

Supplement A: Glossary of a few terms

Authority-based relationships: Relationships where one person is clearly the leader and the other is clearly subordinate. Among the more common structures listed here, this book mostly describes M/s relationships.
- Dominant/submissive (D/s)
- Master/slave (M/s)
- Owner/property (O/p)
- TPE (Total Power Exchange).

Dominant and *submissive* (**Dom** and **sub** or **D-type** and **s-type**) are terms that relate to behaviors linked to personality traits; you could as easily substitute the terms "leader" and "follower."

Dom and Domme: the shorthand male and female version of the word *dominant*. Generally, when I write "Dom" the person can be of either gender. When the topic specifically concerns a female dominant I will use "Domme." In my opinion, the deciding point about whether someone is "dominant" or "domineering" is whether they **expect** service or **accept** service in the context of their role as the dominant leader.

Leather, Leathermen, Leathersex: The Leather subculture is one of many facets of semi-organized alternative sexuality. In recent decades the Leather community has almost come to be viewed as a subset of BDSM culture rather than a descendant of gay culture. Almost anything that is said about Leather and its evolution to present times is subject to challenge, so to avoid controversy I've simply listed some resources in the Supplement so you'll have places to look for more information if you are interested.

Master and slave: usually applied to a 24/7 relationship structure wherein the subordinate person (slave) has surrendered authority over themselves and pledged to serve and to obey another person (commonly called their Master). Master then is said to have authority over this person while providing for this person's wellbeing and spiritual/educational guidance.

Old Guard: A term used for the past few decades to describe a near-mythical time in gay Leather history when returned GIs from World War II blended some features of their military experiences with their kinky interests to produce a subculture that over time became known as "Leather." Some of the distant echoes of their quasi-military rules of protocol, inclusion, and exclusion can still be seen in today's BDSM society.

Submissive versus slave

Note: Once again, I caution readers that the characteristics listed under "submissive" and "slave" are generalizations based on my own research and experiences living within (and studying) the field of BDSM and Master/slave relations since 2001. These descriptions are certainly not intended to be taken as *rules*. These are my own distinctions and may not be generally accepted by others practicing D/s or M/s structures. As you, yourself, grow in BDSM experience, what I write in this book generally—and the following points about distinctions between "submissive" and "slave" specifically—may make more sense to you.

I'll begin by proposing that submissive and slave motivations and behaviors are often quite different. While one is certainly not better than the other, one set of behaviors is more likely to fit some people than others.

submissive
- D/s relationship is based on power exchange (meaning that the submissive who normally has personal authority over what they, themselves, may or may not do or have done to them can give or exchange that power to the Dom/me for a prescribed period)
- Submissives have a strong desire to serve—but under certain negotiated conditions.
- Typically, the negotiated area include the submissive's terms of service, the length of that service, the hard and soft limits, and the safewords.

- The submissive will also negotiate those aspects of their life that the Dom doesn't control. These aspects often include the submissive's biological family and children, work, education and religious observance.
- The conditions under which the submissive is willing to serve can be renegotiated (This is a major issue: the submissive retains the personal authority to ask their Dominant to renegotiate their terms of service, but the Dominant is under no obligation to accept the newly proposed conditions.)
- If the Dom breaks the submissives hard limits, the scene would end and—in the case of a breach of a relationship trust—the relationship could end.
- The Dom may be permitted to break "soft limits" (things the submissive has said they really aren't interested in) after discussing it with the submissive and obtaining their permission.
- In many/most cases, submissives cross back and forth between retaining and surrendering control over some aspect of their lives and continue to make decisions in the areas that are off-limits for their Dom
- A submissive re-submits to the Dom at the start of any scene or activity over which the Dom has negotiated authority. Importantly, the submissive retains the choice as to whether or not to submit to the Dom.

Consensual slave
- M/s relationship is based on authority transfer (This means that once the person who is to become the slave has, in fact, surrendered personal authority over him/herself to their Master/Owner, they no longer have the personal power to make decisions for him/herself. Thus, a slave would not have the authority to enter into a D/s scene with someone other than their Master/Owner without that Master/Owner's specifically transferring THEIR authority over their own slave to another person.)
- At least in theory, the slave gives up all rights to make personal decisions and becomes the "property" of a Master or Owner.
- The core values are service and obedience.
- The slave loses the right to say "no" to Master: in its place, slave may say, "Sir, if it pleases you, Sir" to mean: "Master, I really rather would not do that." or "Sir, only if it pleases you, Sir"

which is as close to "no" as slave is permitted. (Note: Master has an ethical obligation only to push through an "only if" reply so long as Master thinks that doing so remains in the slave's best interest. Requiring a slave to proceed through an "only if" command on Master's whim violates the basic Master/slave pact on Master's part and represents a contract violation.)

- As slave cannot "red out," slave thus has accepted their Master's limits and does what is asked of them regardless of their feelings about it. ("What does 'liking it' have to do with it?")
- In many cases, a slave will give up their rights to personal property and will continue to work for the benefit of Master's household or business.
- A slave's purpose is to make Master's life easier. In that regard, a slave is expected to know Master's wants and likes to the extent that the slave can take independent action on Master's behalf (proactive rather than reactive service; to show initiative as a thinking person)
- If a slave removes their own collar it constitutes withdrawal from the relationship
- May be more interested in taking care of others ("service heart") than in being taken care of ("sorts by others" in psychology-speak)
- May very well be a dominant in most other aspects of their life, but have chosen to be submissive to (or simply to serve) one single person

Switch—common use: someone who enjoys being either the Top or the bottom; enjoys giving or receiving physical SM stimulation. Among Leathermen, activity switches are sometimes referred to as "versatile."

Switch—less common use: someone who is willing to take either the leadership or subordinate role in a relationship depending upon the "chemistry" or "connection" within that particular partner. When used this way, a person is referred to as a **psychological switch**. (Note: while "physical switches" can easily switch within their relationship, "psychological switches" do not. Psychological switches would have relationships wherein their roles are different—dominant in one relationship and subordinate (not necessarily submissive) with the other. This is an advanced and controversial topic and I only touch on it in this book.)

Supplement B: Suggested reading

First, an apology to authors whose works are not listed here. There are so many extraordinarily good books on the market that I've had to force myself to stop listing them, here. These books should only represent a starting point for your further reading.

Books if You're Just Starting Out in BDSM
- Screw the Roses, *Send Me the Thorns: The Romance and Sexual Sorcery of Sadomasochism* by Philip Miller and Molly Devon (*The classic guide to sadomasochism* that is intended to strip away myth, shame, and fear, about BDSM to reveal truths about this intense form of eroticism.)
- *When Someone You Love is Kinky* by Dossie Easton and Catherine Liszt (VERY helpful for explaining your interest and involvement in BDSM to non-kinky family and friends.)
- *Sensuous Magic, 2 Edition: Your guide to S/M for Adventurous Couples* by Patrick Califia (Califia mixes erotic vignettes with practical advice and personal insights to produce a very creative guide to sadomasochism for couples.)
- *Playing Well with Others* by Lee Harrington and Mollena Williams (Interestingly, this book is a marvelous companion to this book that you've been reading. We cover very little ground in common and their material really picks up where this book has left off. And both authors are friends of mine.)
- *The New Topping Book*, by Janet W. Hardy and Dossie Easton (Helps to explain what make someone a "good" dominant, including some of the mental aspects of being a dominant, offers some advice on BDSM play and techniques, and covers the all-important area of safety.
- *The New Bottoming Book*, by Janet W. Hardy and Dossie Easton (The "mate" to the previously-recommended book, this one is written for submissives/bottoms and deals largely with the mental/emotional aspects of being a submissive, rather than hands-on instructions in techniques and toys.)

Books on the Psychological Aspects of BDSM
- *The Control Book* by Peter Masters (One of my favorite books: it's about the fine art of taking control of your partner—the

processes involved, using control, ensuring that you have control, and—importantly—about giving control back once you are done with it. To his vast credit, Masters also discusses how to fix a situation if it goes psychologically wrong.)

- *This Curious Human Phenomenon: An Exploration of Some Uncommonly Explored Aspects of BDSM* by Peter Masters (Masters is one of my heroes. Fabulous author and profound thinker. There is material in this book that you simply won't find addressed by any other author.)
- *Partners in Power: Living in Kinky Relationships* by Jack Rinella (A "must read" before you start a D/s relationship. It addresses the question: "Is it possible to form lasting, healthy, loving relationships that are based on power, control and pain?)
- *The Master's Manual: A Handbook of Erotic Dominance* by Jack Rinella (Another "must read"—particularly if you're starting down the "Master/slave" path.)

Core Readings for Master/slave

- *Ask the man who Owns Him* by David Stein with David Schachter (Interviews with long-term gay Master/slave couples: demonstrates the wide variety of approaches to hierarchical relationship structures.)
- *Leading and Supporting Love* by Chris M. Lyon (Only book in print that describes workable ways to establish and maintain hierarchical relationships that are mutually supportive. Very sophisticated yet easy to read.)
- *Master/slave Relations: Handbook of Theory and Practice* by Robert J Rubel (This will provide your best opportunity to get an overall understanding of Master/slave relationships— especially about things to think about before starting one and techniques for maintaining such a structure once you're in one.)
- *Protocol Handbook for the Female slave: Handbook of Theory and Practice* by Robert J Rubel (An actual slave's protocol manual, this gives ample examples of protocols that can be modified for your particular relationship.)
- *Master/slave Relations: Communications 401—the advanced course* by Robert J. Rubel (Out-of-the-box communications book that provides a wide range of work-arounds to often-hidden communication challenges.)

- *Paradigms of Power: Styles of M/s relationships* Edited by Raven Kaldera (all Raven's works are "Must-Reads" in my view.
- *SlaveCraft: Roadmaps for Erotic Servitude—Principles, Skills and Tools* by Guy Baldwin (Profound and masterful book discussing the philosophy and practice of service.
- *Real Service* by Joushua Tenpenny and Raven Kladera (A "must read" if you're thinking of preparing a manual of protocols for your slave.)
- *Dear Raven and Joshua Questions and Answers About Master/ Slave Relationships* by Raven Kaldera and Joshua Tenpenny (Read this before you establish your D/s or M/s relationship: it will save you a world of hurt.)
- *Analyzing Performance Problems: Or, You Really Oughta Wanna—How to Figure out Why People Aren't Doing What They Should Be, and What to do About It*, by Robert Mager and Peter Pipe (Another "must read" when developing a training program for your slave.)

Books about the Leather Culture

- *The Leatherman's Handbook* by Larry Townsend. (Published in 1972, this was the first book to write out the codes of conduct that the underground Leather scene and SM play that gay Leathermen lived by. This is the basic book on this subject.)
- *Urban Aboriginals* by Geoff Mains (This book explores the spiritual, sexual, emotional, cultural, and physiological aspects that make this "scene" one of the most prominent yet misunderstood subcultures in our society.)
- *Ties That Bind: The SM/Leather/Fetish Erotic Style: Issues, Commentaries and Advice* by Guy Baldwin (A practicing psychologist and one of the most important thinkers on subjects of SM/leather/fetish erotic style, this is a "must read" book covering relationship issues, the Leather community, the SM experience, and personal transformation, as they relate to this form of erotic play).
- *Leathersex: Your guide for the Curious Outsider and the Serious Player* by Joseph Bean (Another of the basic books about Leather by one of the most knowledgeable and lucid writers to tackle the topic.)

Other Books that I Recommend Highly
- *Living M/s: A Book for Masters, slaves, and Their Relationships* by Dan and Dawn Williams (Good friends and a great book for those interested in the realities of living daily in a Master/slave structure)
- *The Ultimate Guide to Kink: BDSM, Role Play and the Erotic Edge* by Tristan Taormino (This is a marvelous collection of seriously sophisticated essays ranging from expert how-to tutorials to thought-provoking essays addressing complex questions about desire, power, and pleasure. The essays are written by extremely well known national presenters who are sexuality and/or BDSM educators.)

Definitive History of the Origins of BDSM
For a definitive historical discussion of the origins of BDSM both in Europe and in the US, see Robert Bienvenu's doctoral dissertation: *The Development of Sadomasochism as a Cultural Style in the Twentieth-Century* United States. Unfortunately, this dissertation is available only from libraries or from a PDF copy that has been passed from person to person.

Books about Leather Spirituality
- *Sacred Kink* by Lee Harrington
- *It's Not About the Whip: Love, Sex, and Spirituality in the BDSM Scene* by Sensuous Sadie
- Anything by Raven Kaldera and Joshua Tenpenny:
  - *Sacred Power, Holy Surrender*
  - *Dark Moon Rising: Pagan BDSM & the Ordeal Path*
  - *The Ethical Psychic Vampire* (This one is about "energy play" and is in a league of its own.)

Books about Asperger Syndrome–High-functioning Autism
This is a list of books on Asperger Syndrome that I've personally found very helpful.
- *22 Things a Woman Must Know: If She Loves a Man With Asperger's Syndrome* by Rudy Simone
- *Alone Together* by Katrin Bentley
- *The Unwritten Rules of Social Relationships: Decoding Social*

Mysteries Through the Unique Perspectives of Autism by Temple Grandin and Sean Barron
- *The Journal of Best Practices: A Memoir of Marriage, Asperger Syndrome, and One Man's Quest to Be a Better Husband* by David Finch

Supplement C: Where to find information

Lists:
- Of practically every kink known to man—just in case you thought you'd heard it all: everything2.com/title/Submissive+BDSM+Play+Partner+Check+List
- Glossary of BDSM terms: www.xeromag.com/fvbdglossary.html

Major general information resource sites:
- www.FetLife.com: "Fet," as it is called, is THE go-to source for just about anything these days. It is the "Facebook" for kinksters. There are discussion groups for just about any topic you can think of. It's my first stop for anything I'm researching. (Thanks, John Baku, for creating this Website.)
- bannon.com: the site that is both 100% authoritative and responsible. Race Bannon, author of *Learning The Ropes: A Basic Guide to Safe and Fun BDSM Lovemaking* not only sends you to responsible sites but also provides some guidance about what to be looking for and avoiding when it comes to Internet searches concerning BDSM and Leather.
- HUGE and extremely useful site for all things submissive: www.submissiveguide.com
- High quality information: *www.the-iron-gate.com*
- One of the most comprehensive and sophisticated sites I can recommend—particularly for types of play and the psychology of play—belongs to Peter Masters (Sydney, AU). Clever guy. www.peter-masters.com/wiki/index.php/The_Control_Book

Major Master/slave resource:
MAsT International is the overarching organization for those of us interested in such authority-based relationships. Their Website is: http://www.mast.net

As you can read from their homepage, "Masters And slaves Together International (MAsT) is an association of individuals interested in engaging in personal relationships that are based upon the conscious exchange of power and authority. MAsT believes that such relationships can be a valid path to authenticity, self-actualization, and happiness for such individuals, and MAsT is therefore dedicated to equipping them with tools and resources that will assist them in developing relationships that are healthy, functional, and real."

Interest in structured relationships has grown dramatically in recent years.

As a measure, just look at the growth of local chapters of MAsT (Masters And slaves Together). Here are the stats showing the number of chapters per year and overall MAsT membership according to (and with thanks to) Master Bob Blount (Executive Director of MAsT International):

Year	Number of Chapters	Total MAsT Membership
2007	38	700
2008	49	784
2009	67	1,206
2010	76	1,396
2011	86	1,550
2012	112	2,552

Some of my favorite special-interest sites:
- Spirituality and BDSM—particularly Leather spirituality: duskpeterson.com/leatherculture/spirituality/links.htm
- Sex and sexuality topics—extensive site: www.sexuality.org/books.html
- Leather news and views: www.leatherati.com/leatherati_issues/2011/09/switzerland-no-more.html

Outstanding sites with lots of information:
- collarncuffs.com/resources/doku.php

- *www.denversub.com/bdsm.html*
- *www.domsub.info/communityarticles.shtml*
- *www.frugaldomme.com/dangers/*
- *www.idahobdsm.com/articles.html*

Calendar of events–weekend conferences
- *www.thebdsmeventspage.com/index.html*

Online BDSM education
- sexedforadults.org Disclaimer: I'm a member of the faculty for this site. This is a very professional site that offers both fee-based and free classes and webinars, extensive courses, and one-on-one coaching. The faculty are seasoned authors or recognized educators.

Master/slave Conferences
Over the past few years, weekend conferences have evolved that feature Master/slave relations over BDSM activities. Concurrently, there are competitions held at these conferences for Master/slave titles that represent specific regions. Winners of regional titles compete for the International Master/slave title at South Plains Leatherfest in Dallas in March. Here are the related Website links.

Feeder Conferences
[Note: conferences are listed in order of occurrence after Southplains in March. Thus, the Southwest conference appears last because it occurs in January—at the end of the competition cycle for the previous year.]
- **Northwest Leather Celebration** (May, San Jose, CA) *http://www.northwestleathercelebration.com/home*
- **Southeast Leather Fest** (June, Atlanta, GA) *https://secure.seleatherfest.com*
- **Great Lakes Leather Alliance** (Indianapolis, August) *http://greatlakesleather.org/web/schedule.html*
- **Master/slave Conference** (Washington, D.C., September) *http://www.masterslaveconference.org*
- **Southwest Leather Converence** (Phoenix, January) *www.southwestleather.org*

Culminating Event
International Master/slave Conference (Dallas, March)
http://www.southplainsleatherfest.com

Supplement D: Acknowledgments

I particularly want to thank my partner and Owner, M. Jen Fairfield, for her extensive help and support during the many months that it has taken to complete this work. This book could not possibly be what it now has become without her extensive guidance and profound understanding of BDSM in general and authority-based relationships in particular.

As often as not, Jen influenced and shaped the ideas that now comprise this book. In order to become an expert in this field, she read dozens of books by virtually every authority in this area of expertise in order to find and to pass on to me some of the important supporting information that has rounded out this work. Also, she takes great notes in BDSM classes at weekend conferences.

In addition to helping me with content and flow, Jen made sure that I had the time I needed to write this book—an important gift, considering how hectic our lives are. Without her support at every turn I'd never have completed it. Jen was also responsible for overseeing the layout and cover design of this book.

Supplements E: About the Authors

Robet J. Rubel, Ph.D.
Robert Rubel (Dr. Bob), author, educator and photographer is an educational sociologist and researcher by training. He currently has 10 books in print and two DVDs (Books: four on Master/slave topics, two on advanced sex techniques, one on fire play, and three erotic art photo books. DVDs: fire play and beginning impact play).

The recipient of the 2008 Pantheon of Leather's Community Choice Award (man), Dr. Bob has been involved in the BDSM and Total Power Exchange (TPE) scene since the summer of 2001, throwing himself into the literature of the field as though it were an academic study. He presents, judges, and sells his books at weekend kink conferences throughout the year.

Now starting his 70s, Bob has had three long-term relationships: a 17-year marriage, a 14-year marriage, and a 10-year Owner/property relationship in which after two years his Owner gave him his own slave. The three of them remained together for eight more years. In his current relationship, he serves Jen, his Domme and Owner.

Publications
Books on Master/slave Relations
- *Master/slave Relations: Handbook of Theory and Practice.* Las Vegas: Nazca Plains, 2006.
- *Protocols; Handbook for the female slave, second edition.* Las Vegas: Nazca Plains, 2007.
- *Protocol Handbook for the Leather Slave: Theory and Practice.* Las Vegas: Nazca Plains, 2006. (The gender-neutral version of the prior book—same content.)
- *Master/slave Relations: Communications 401—The Advanced Course.* Las Vegas: Nazca Plains, 2007.
- *Master/slave Relations: Solutions 402 – Living in Harmony.* Las Vegas: Nazca Plains, 2007.

Books Other BDSM Topics
- *Flames of Passion: Handbook of Erotic Fire Play.* Las Vegas: Nazca Plains, 2006.

SMTech Book+DVD Combinations
- *Fire Play: A Safety Training Course* (70-minute DVD plus 48-page book) Las Vegas: Nazca Plains, 2012
- *Impact Play 101: Building Your Skills* (70-minute DVD plus 48-page book) Las Vegas: Nazca Plains, 2012

Books on Advanced Sexual Practices
- *Squirms, Screams, and Squirts: Handbook for going from great sex to extraordinary sex.* Las Vegas: Nazca Plains, 2007.
- *Squirms, Screams, and Squirts: The Workbook.* Las Vegas: Nazca Plains, 2010.
- *Screams of Pleasure: Guide for Extraordinary Sex for those with Erectile Dysfunction* (Slightly revised version of Squirms, Screams, and Squirts) (2009)

Books of Erotic and Fetish Art
Three books on erotic and fetish photography titled (with an eye towards perverse humor):
- *Parts: The Erotic Photographic Art of Robert J. Rubel, PhD.* Las Vegas: Nazca Plains, 2006.
- *Wholes: The Erotic Photographic Art of Robert J. Rubel, PhD.* Las Vegas: Nazca Plains, 2006.
- *Holes: The Erotic Photographic Art of Robert J. Rubel, PhD.* Las Vegas: Nazca Plains, 2006.

Edited Publications
Bob served as the Managing Editor of **Power Exchange Magazine** in 2007–2008. Issue Themes
- Master/slave Relations—male Master
- Master/slave Relations—female Master
- Bootblacking
- FemDomme
- Pony Play
- Polyamory
- Daddy/boy
- Leather Spirituality
- Pup/Trainer

In 2007 Bob made a marketing decision and transformed *Power Exchange Magazine* into a small book format. This series, **Power Exchange Books' Resource Series**, are 100-page books on focused topics of interest to BDSM or Leather folk. The series is about the *why* of what we do, not the *how* of it. Book titles include:
- *Playing with Disabilities*
- *The Art of Slavery*
- *Protocols: A Variety of Views*
- *Rope, Bondage, and Power*
- *Age Play*

M. Jen Fairfield
Jen is Dr. Bob's Master. She has extensive experience managing authority-imbalanced relationships. Her D/s experience began in 1992 as she dipped her toe in the water with a nurturing Mommy/boy relationship. Seeking more control than the Mommy/boy relationship could offer, Jen ended that relationship after a year and—following a year of introspection and personal clarification—entered a full-blown D/s relationship that she ran for another 16 years.

Jen found her home in the Leather Master/slave culture in the fall of 2010 and has embraced her calling as a Leather woman—to live a mindful and purpose-driven life with a partner (or partners) who are willing to hold themselves to exacting moral and ethical standards.

Jen has been attending conferences and workshops, reading books, and working closely with Dr. Bob as he has been researching and writing books and making presentations all over the U.S. and Canada. Over the last year, Jen has developed a growing number of presentations that are separate from Bob's.

Currently, Jen and Dr. Bob have books at various points of completion. At this point, their working titles are:

- *BDSM Mastery–Relationships: a guide for creating mindful relationships for Dominants and* (Book Two in the BDSM Mastery Series)
- *Master/slave Mastery: Refining the fire—ideas that matter* (Book Two in the Master/slave Mastery Series)
- *BDSM Mastery—Sex: your guide for erotically adventuresome nights*

Robert J. Rubel
and
M. Jen Fairfield

Jen and Dr. Bob have partnered for presentations at Leather and BDSM Conferences both in the United States and Canada. They host a bi-monthly webinar called An Evening With Jen and Dr. Bob that covers both power-imbalanced relationship issues and also a range of kinky topics.

Jen and Dr. Bob bring their strengths (and weaknesses) to their work, sharing their life experiences and their passion for education.

You can follow Jen and Bob at www.KinkMastery.com where they share interesting kinky images (that Dr. Bob has taken), resources to aid you on your kinky journey, and ideas you may not have thought of. You'll find a range of (perhaps) new thoughts and ideas that go beyond the World of Kink. You'll also find their presentation calendar and schedule of publication dates for future books.

If you'd like to join their bi-monthly free webinar discussions, you can register at: www.CreativeSexuality.org. Just sign in to the "free online events" tab and click on: "An Evening with Jen and Dr. Bob," and then click on "get e-mailed reminders."

www.KinkMastery.com

Creative Studio

Made in the USA
San Bernardino,
CA